FAR SIDE OF THE SEA

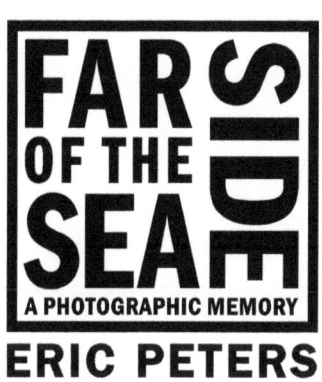

FAR SIDE OF THE SEA

A PHOTOGRAPHIC MEMORY

ERIC PETERS

To Danielle:
A strong, brave, resilient friend.

"There is a fragrance in the air, a certain passage of a song, an old photograph falling out from the pages of a book, the sound of somebody's voice in the hall that makes your heart leap and fills your eyes with tears. Who can say when or how it will be that something easters up out of the dimness to remind us of a time before we were born and after we will die?"

—Frederick Buechner, *Telling The Truth*

INTRODUCTION

You've seen them too: abandoned objects, unnoticed people, castoff relics. Rejected, forgotten, covered in mud and rust, alienated, cast aside, no longer needed in the world. In a repurposed kingdom, nothing and no one is lost or forgotten forever. In keeping secrets, we tell and retell lies, self-protect, tether ourselves to shame, and avoid vulnerability as inconsequential, weak, or irrelevant. A worthy character, Vulnerability is a good, strong companion for times like this. A loyal teacher, she is worth walking arm-in-arm with.

Far Side Of The Sea is, as best I can figure, a work of fictional biography. The narratives are invented, but as with any creation, a part of the creator indwells the work. While thumbing through a stack of black-and-white prints I shot over the course of the past twenty-five years, I happened upon one of a botanical garden gate. It made me think of Adam and Eve, their Garden, on the outside now looking in. The imagery of that photo prompted me to write an accompanying vignette, and encouraged by what the exercise evoked, I wrote the book you now hold in your hands.

I've never met a soul who wants to feel alone in the world, who wants to be discarded, who wants to have no purpose or meaning. Maybe you, like me, will find an unexpected camaraderie with the objects and castaway souls in these pages. Don't miss their vulnerability, for their stories, after all, are also our own.

Hardly memorable except for being forgettable, the overlooked objects of earth bear decay as scars of experience, persistence, disappointment, and, not least of all, courage.

In the slow, persevering cadence of endurance, they testify. Have eyes to see, and ears to hear. Do not ignore their vanquished dreams or fail to imagine their memories, etched like corrosion into skeleton hopes, for theirs, like ours, are stories in need of telling.

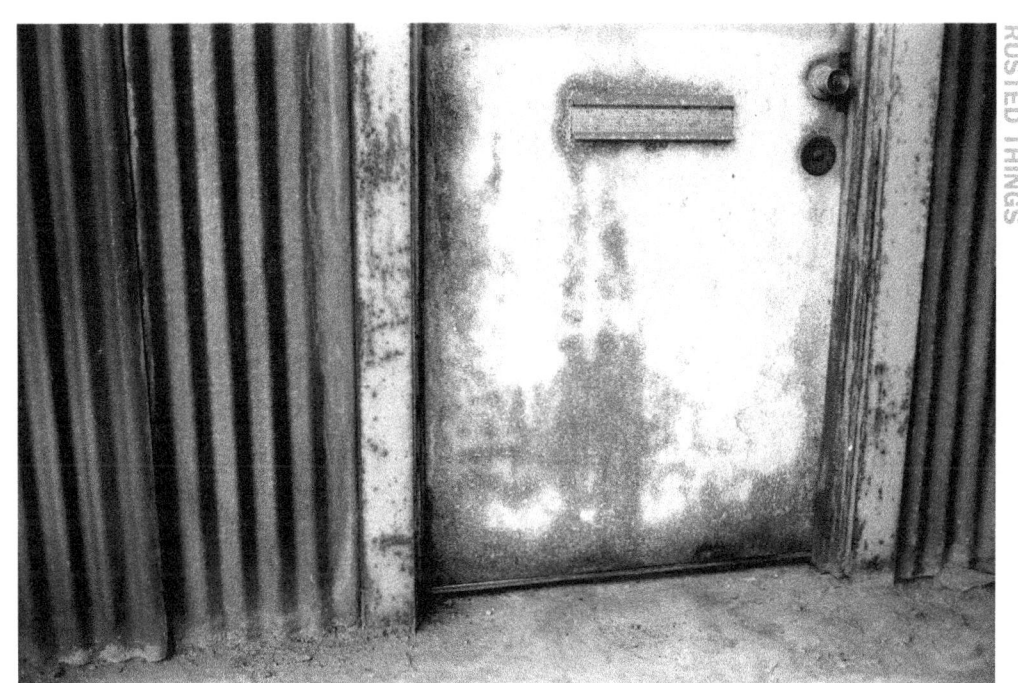

Location Unknown   Yashica 35mm

I am a limping ruin. Darkness is shuttered inside me. One day the shutters will be ripped away, and light will summon forth the life still alive within. I will not limp forever.

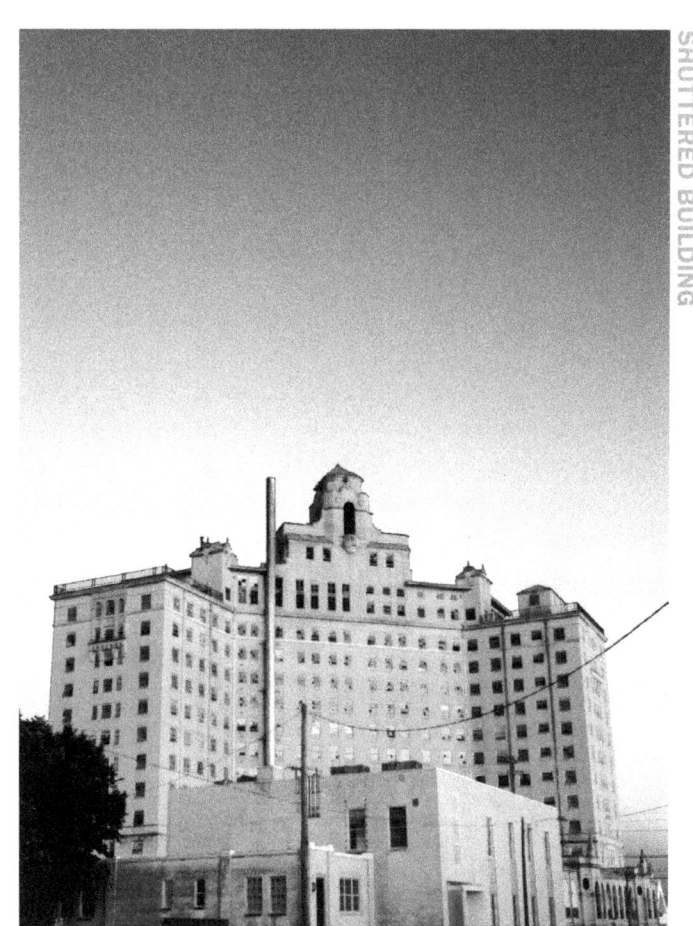

Mineral Wells, Texas   iPhone

The comet passed like an arrow through earth's core and continued arcing into forever. The world is aloof. At its pole a man walks high on a wire, arms outstretched, a Wallenda balancing act with no safety net. He has struggled up the tight wire for an eternity, and at last stakes claim over the realm below. Angels flare from outstretched meridians, lighting the infinite way, and earth heralds the crowning event.

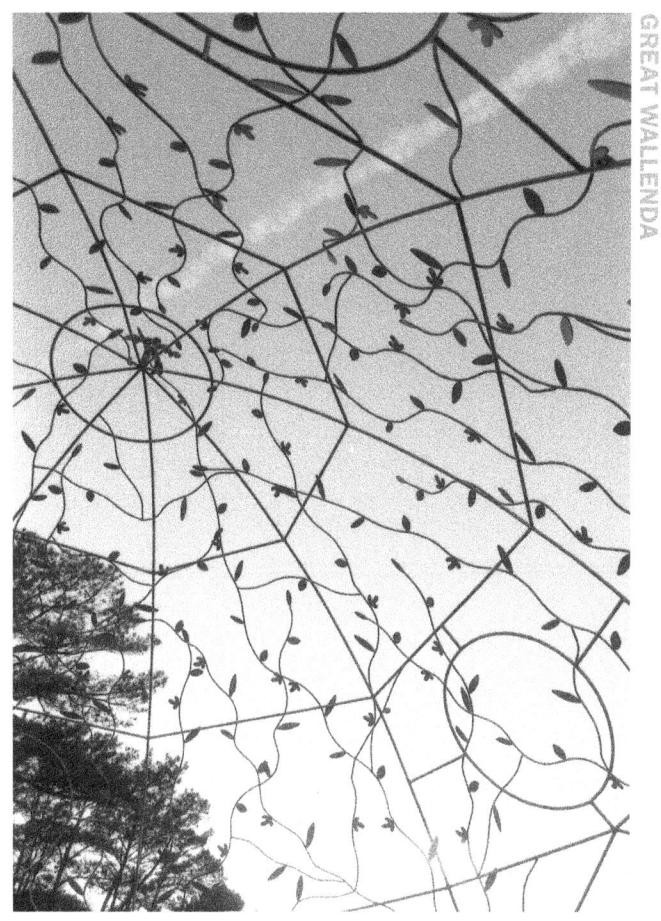

Birmingham, Alabama   Yashica 35mm

I am an invitation into the holy of holies. Inside, men of mortal sin, both outward and hidden alike, greet one another, partake of the sacraments together, each doing his best to acknowledge the restlessness stirring inside him, or to stir the apathy resting there. The body has many parts, many roles; I play mine.

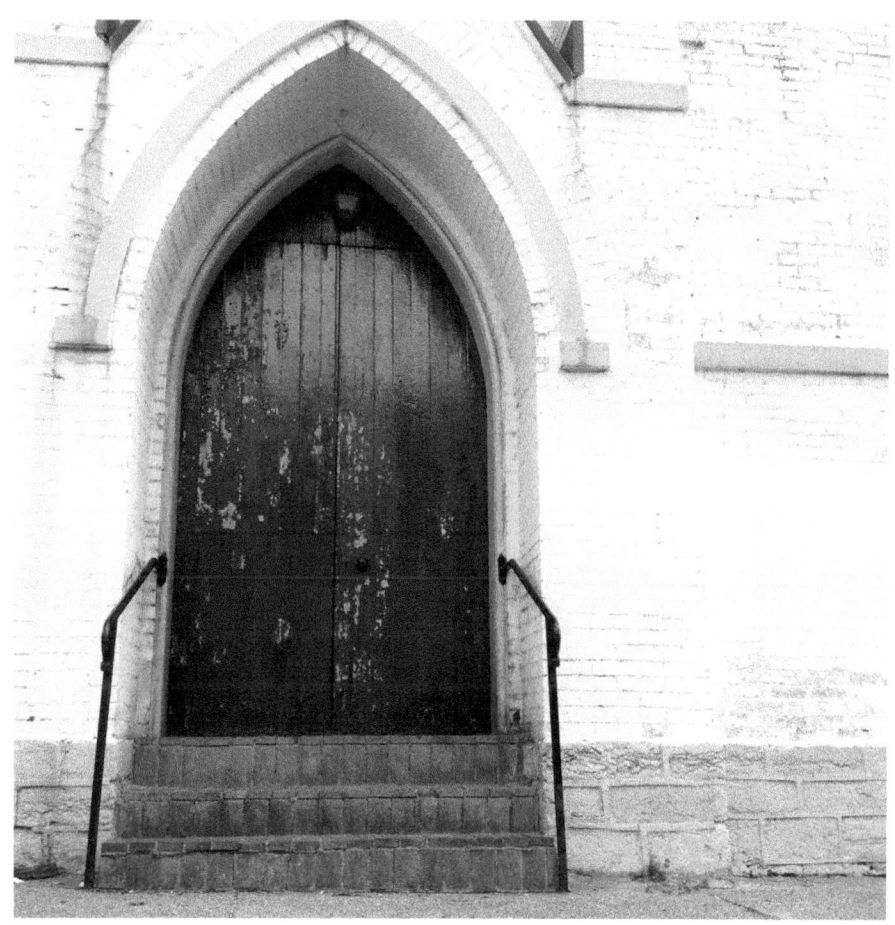

Lexington, Kentucky   iPhone

He cannot explain what happens when he presses his fingers to the keys. Something overwhelms him, as if he is merely the second man alive in his own skin. He can no more dismiss the gift and the need to express it than he can ignore the second man reverberating inside his own soul.

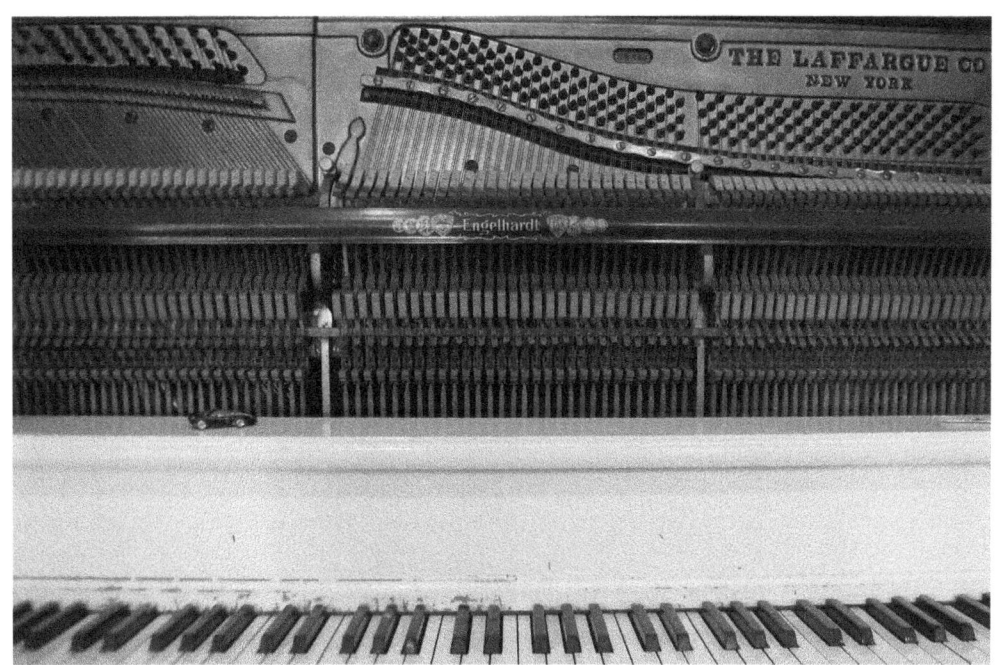

Nashville, Tennessee

Nikon D40

Every so often I walk past the place, my old stomping ground. Peeking through the gate, the aroma of rhododendron and jasmine greets me. In there, the days were good. There was an air of permanence. To think, I traded it all for an apple of power and my own confederacy. It seems a lifetime ago, for I can no longer recall the finer details—either that, or I've chosen to forget them entirely. Out here, nothing works and nothing lasts. The edges blur and vignette. Everything goes wrong, and, if it hasn't already, dies. Nothing is permanent. I want the ache and recollection of that idyllic place stricken from my memory, and yet—

I hope I never forget it.

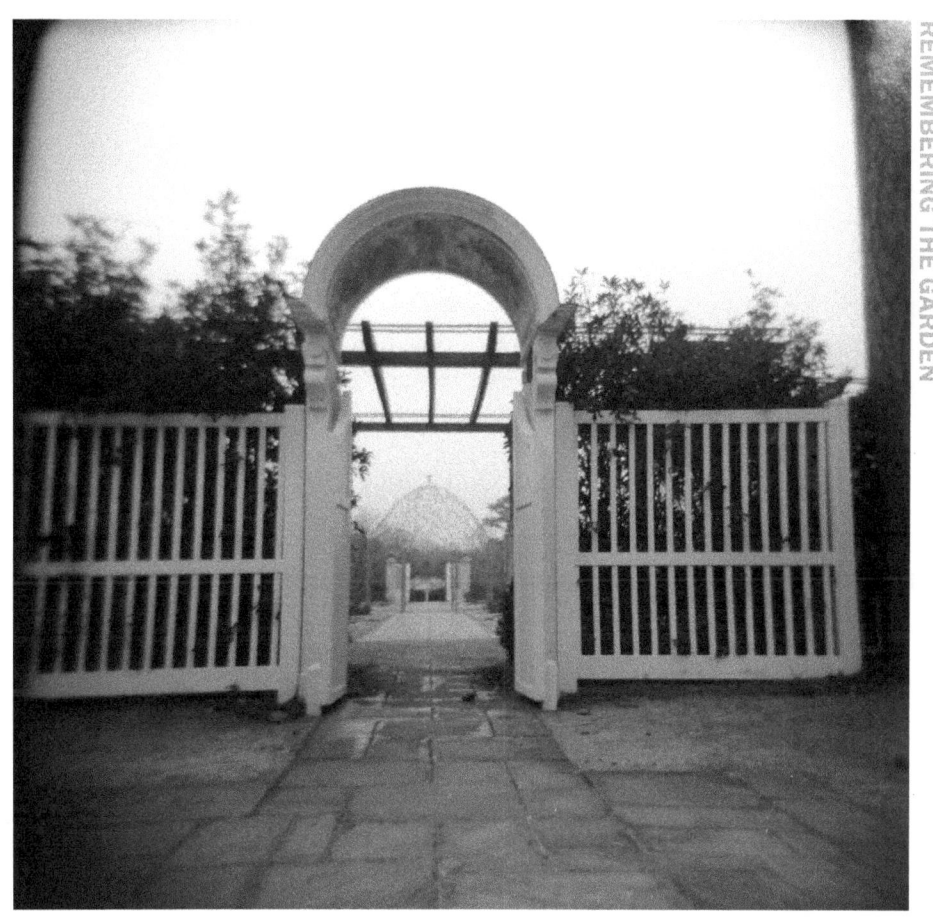

Birmingham, Alabama   Holga 120S

Eighty-eight was a summer for the record books. Soil baked and split open, crops withered, children's plastic toys melted, tires dry-rotted, and the color green disappeared from earth. A four-wheeled convection oven, my vinyl seats were veritable grills for anyone foolish enough to sit on them barelegged. My steering wheel, its cracked and brittle skin bearing the brunt of sunlight, was a ring of fire potent to any pilgrim hand gripping it. My dash glowed. Chrome shimmered. And time, as a matter of telling, stopped in its tracks.

Many hands have gripped me over the years, as the good Lord and Wolfsburg Castle emblem attest. Facing head-on the oncoming twists and dead-man curves, the pilgrim's hope is that at precisely the right moment, the will of God shall be—is being—done, and the Kingdom shall appear and remain until time, as a matter of telling and being told, is no longer necessary.

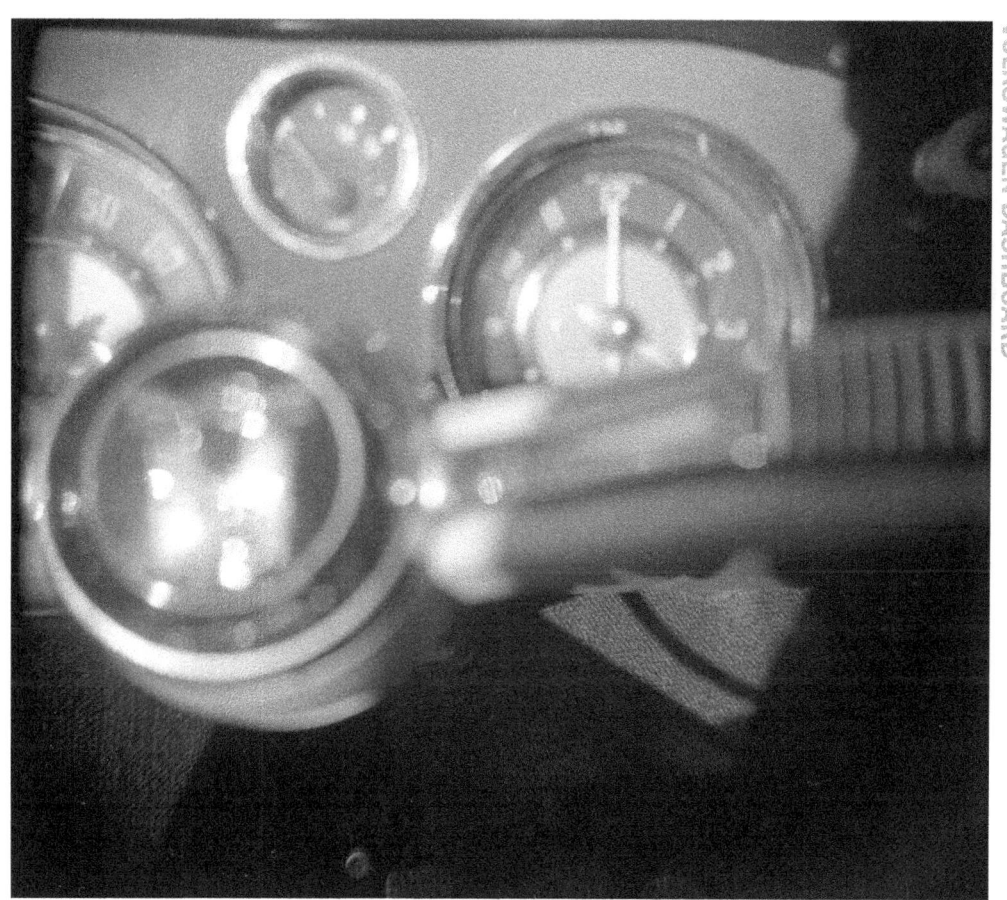

Rising Star, Texas   Holga 120S

From these heights, anything is possible. Having at last snapped in the mental anguish and isolation of his own torment, a madman sniper could just as easily inflict mortal damage on unsuspecting passers-by as could a desperate woman hurl herself down onto the hell below. Great and terrible things happen. Too much is seen; too little is forgotten.

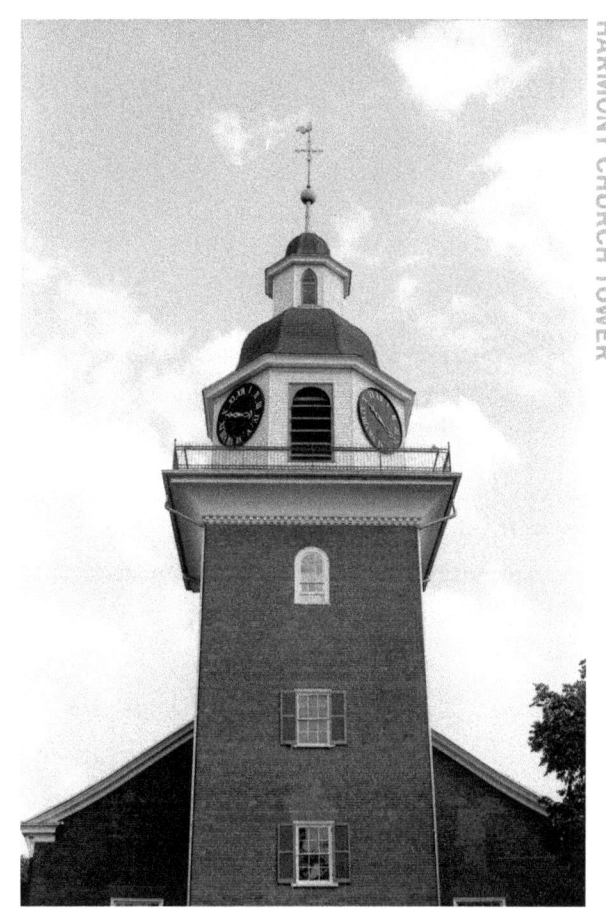

Old Economy Village, Pennsylvania   Yashica 35mm

Not unlike a weed, I sprung eagerly from the ground. Rather than hack me down, a thoughtful and observant steward recognized my juvenile clusters, leaving me to cling to the nearby columns to climb, mature, aspire, and struggle.

Long-leaf pines tower overhead, carelessly littering their spoked vengeance on the ground below. For the most part, the trees and I get along. Rooted in the world, we tolerate one another's eccentricities, respect one another's struggle to earn the sun's broad attention, and yet each day we receive what we need.

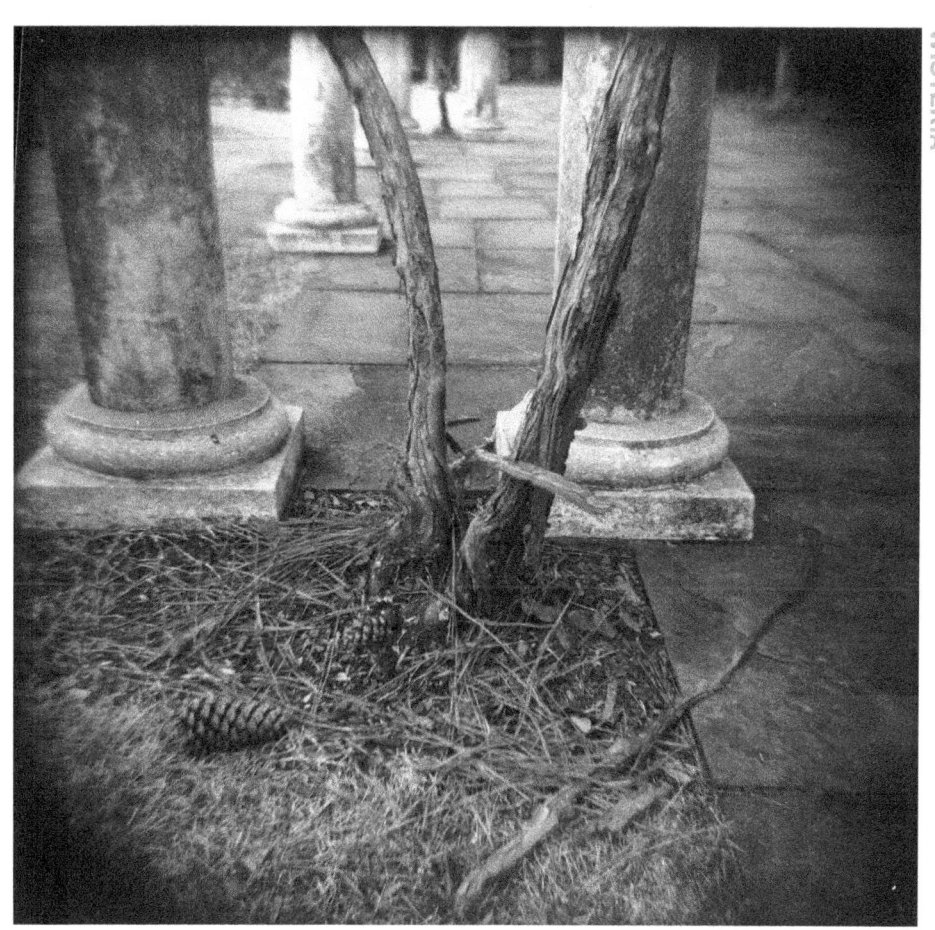

Birmingham, Alabama

Holga 120S

No one knows why we were spared. Laid down when the day was done, brothers fell broken, unnoticed, trampled into the earth, never to be seen again. Flanks aligned in orderly rank and file, a brigade on the brink of engagement, we were held in permanent reserve, never to realize what we were sure would be our glory. Settling amid russet hues, scarred expressions, and elusive purpose, time settles on us, hope dims, and we lose our way.

Though lost, may we yet find contentment in surprisingly creative, meek, utilitarian ways. Preparing the way like that Baptist John, we serve mortals, guiding them from Point A to Point B. Lost ourselves, perhaps we rediscover our way by stewarding obscurity. Here, nothing and nobody is lost forever.

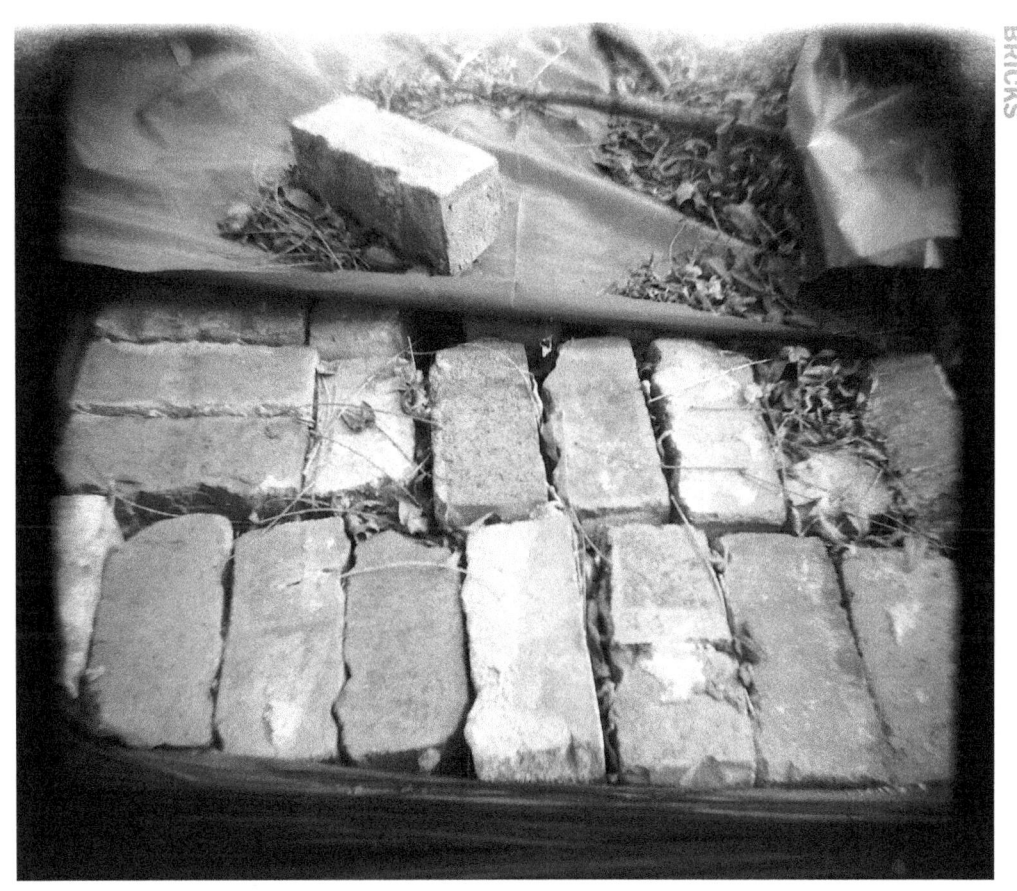

Camdenton, Missouri

Holga 120S

I thought of him alone with his oils, half-finished starry nights and wheat fields, the unrelenting legions of despondency and awful dialogue—and tired, stubbled, sunburned Vincent believing the diatribe as it railed against him.

I wondered if that passionate, destitute, overlooked soul could comprehend his worth in the world. Did he own any hope that his impasto heart, the thick swabs of Cobalt blue and confessional ochres, the gilt moons, the birds—my God, those crows!—and the many slants of light would one day shine into countless souls who would be just as much in need of that gravity and radiance?

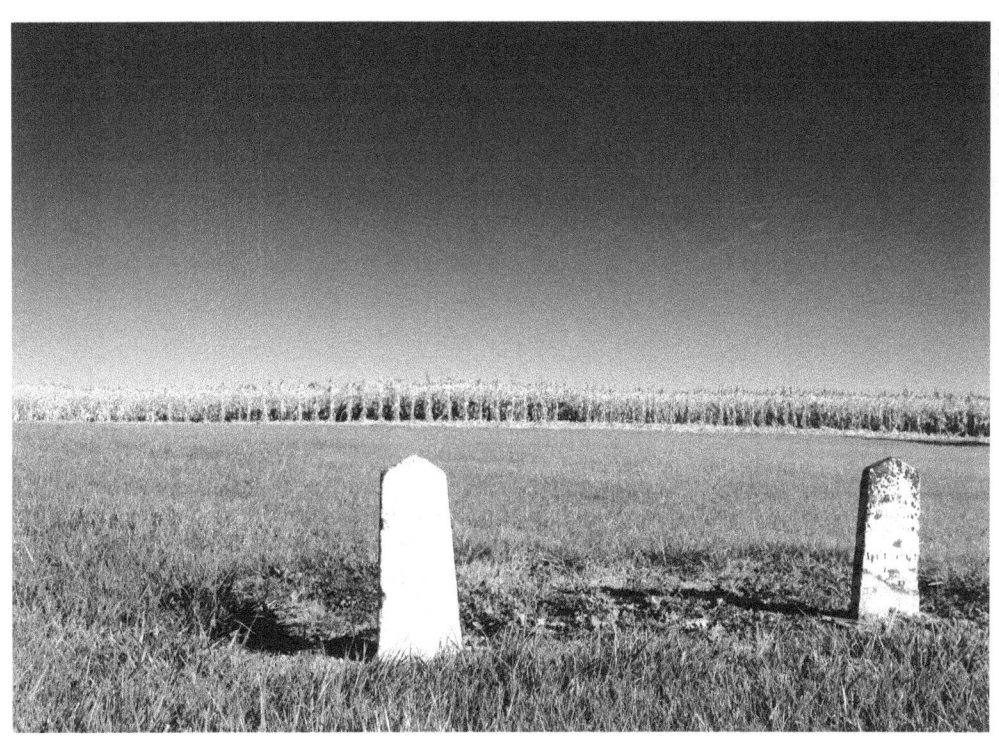

Vicinity Richmond, Indiana

iPhone

The wind has no regrets. On this hill, the still and silence are neither still nor silent for long. The trees are bony magician fingers reaching upward, their long shadows bruised and blushing. Earth attempts to drag itself free from the cold, submerged confinement of a long obedience. Up here, the wind does not whisper; it wails. I should know; crowning the hill, absorbing every blow, I am an altar, a token in the world.

On two forward columns I sit regal and alert, a lion presiding over realm. I have witnessed the rise and fall of lives, seasons, suns, spinning heavens—I remember them all. Where I have languished beneath a listless sky, I have also been transformed by tomorrow as it rises from a dead horizon. I have consumed light and I have given it. I am lit from without, and lit from within.

The rambunctious wind, its ghosts circling about, assails me, begs me to forget, to cease remembering, to abandon my charge as a token marking the place to which God has brought me.

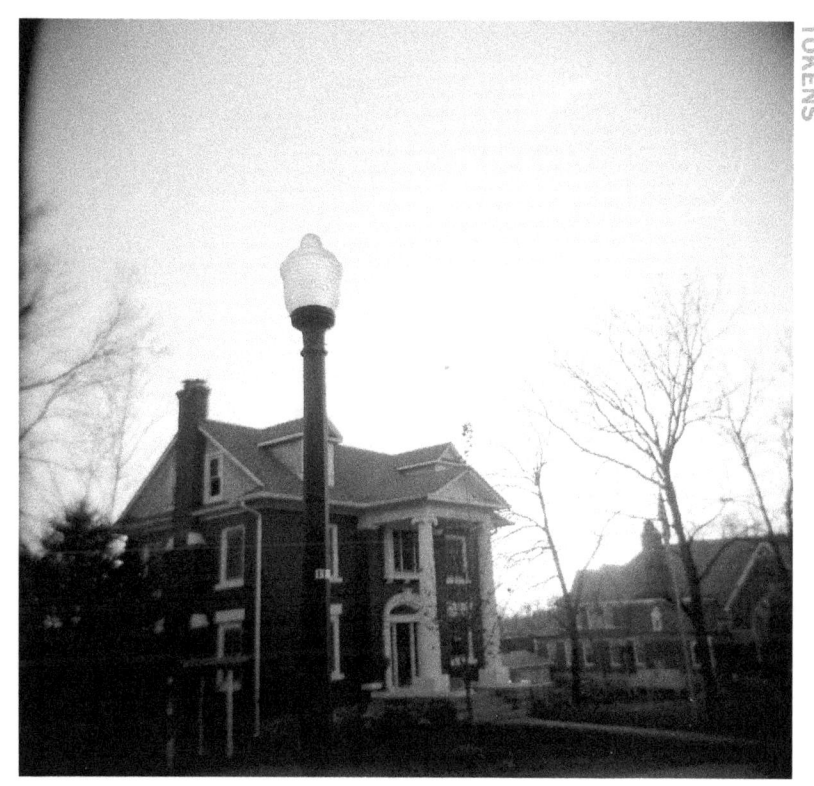

Liberty, Missouri   Holga 120S

I was a stolen seed stealing purchase in a narrow ribbon of inhospitable earth. Except for delivery trucks and the occasional patron seeking a covert parking spot, it was a lonesome existence here in the unfrequented alley between ramshackle, helter-skelter warehouses. Not until late morning did the sun peek above the roofline crest, and by then songbirds had mostly gone silent. When the sun's direct rays finally managed to reach this spot, it was a most welcome tickle on my uppermost extremities. Like any good thing, it was worth the wait.

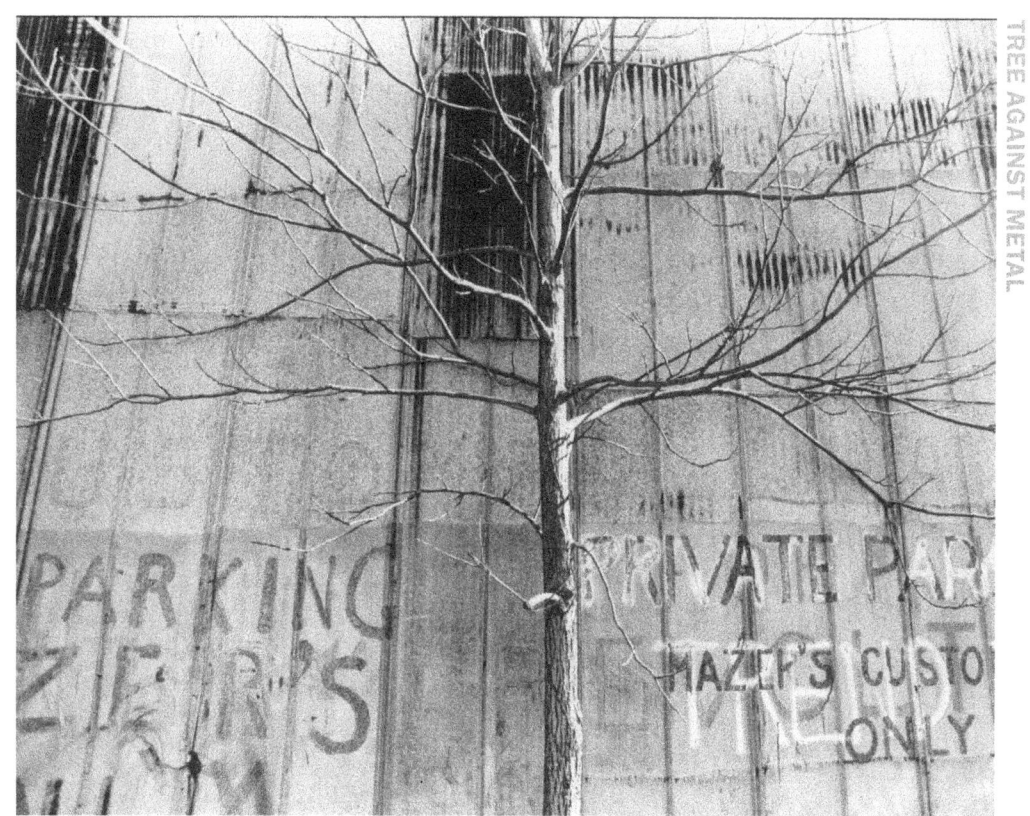

Homewood, Alabama

Yashica 35mm

I remember the last time someone paused here. The sun was draped behind a massive summer cloud, a soul came hobbling, and I, in my true, tender vocation, offered them rest. It was enough for me, and I for them.

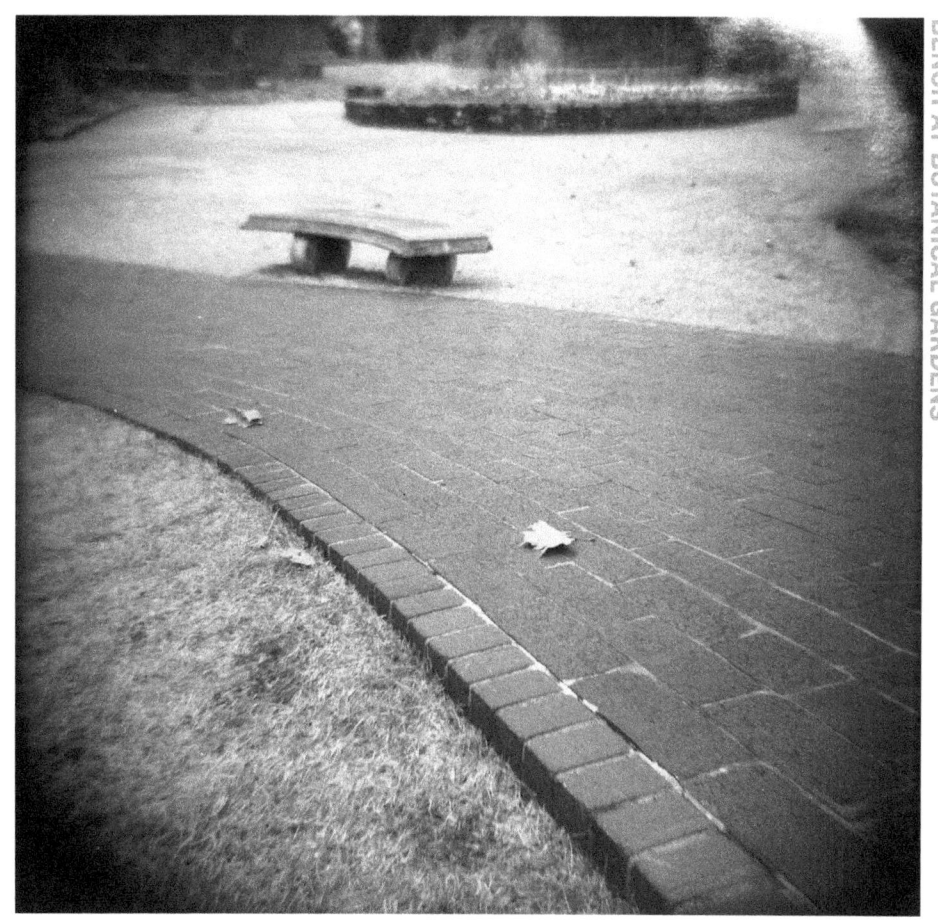

Birmingham, Alabama

Holga 120S

Among my traits, I count a shy demeanor, a slight if not perpetual grin, a meager interior, and a plebeian heart that is not humble enough. Utterly lacking in modernity, I push forward as much as my small engine will propel me.

Stars whiplash the night sky. Heaven pardons their constant interruptions. Hope having long since lapsed, the days having deteriorated into repetitive murmurs, a sad pall of insignificance suffocated my 1200cc spirit. I forget how long I stood crypt-like among the belly-tickling weeds and insufferable field mice, but something like scales fell from my rusted eyes the day a passing stranger caught me out of the corner of his eager eye, and seeing something good and desirable in me, claimed me as his own. Unexpectedly, my stalled soul reignited. To this I owe everything. There is still a place in the world for unwanted things.

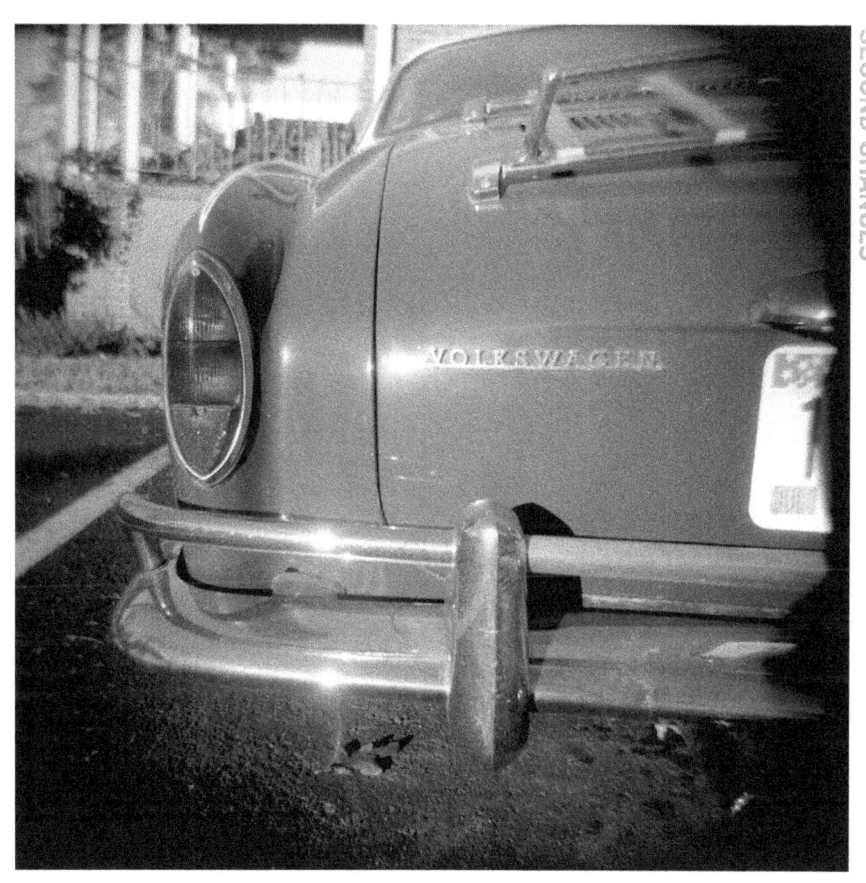

Birmingham, Alabama   Holga 120S

On late summer afternoons, we retire to the patio where Evelyn has prepared sweet tea and a Dixie plate of saltines and extra-sharp cheddar cheese. We lay towels on the chairs, still cruel with heat, to avoid scalding our wrinkled hamstrings. Gray shadows rise behind us, and we lose ourselves to technicolor memories—"My God, how on earth did we take that place for granted?"

On the heels of our debacle, reality necessitated the construction of adequate living quarters. Coming to grips with our situation—rather, it gripping us—and moving past the shock of dismissal and fall from grace, we chose a suitable plot of land within sight of our former paradise. One of the first nights, the thunder of a storm shook the walls and our bones. For the first time, that earth-enveloping sound scared us to death. Rain was nothing new—but fear was.

Out here, everything breaks, tools rust, the earth temporarily accepts the living. Surrounded by interminable weeds and a deep awareness of not being enough, I work my fields of furrowed grief. Out here, work is nothing new—but the ache is.

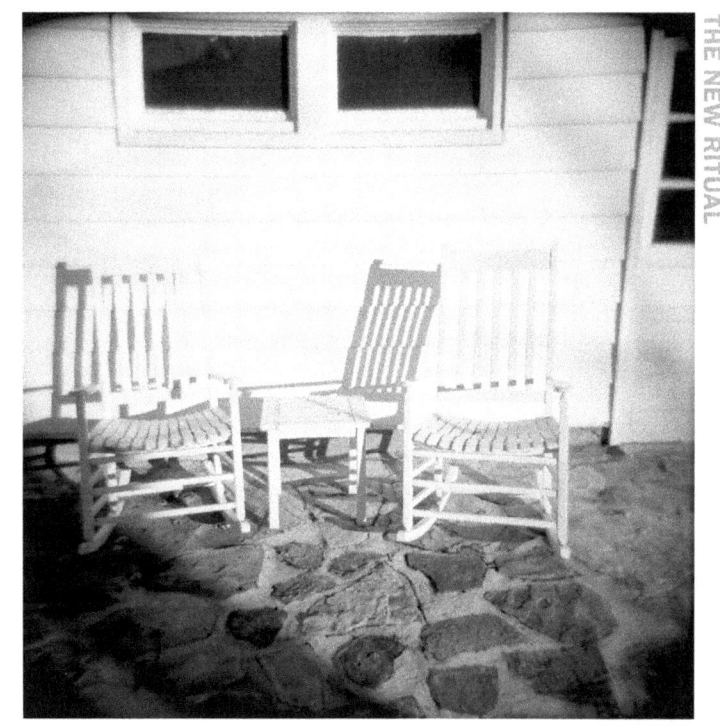

St. Charles, Missouri   Holga 120S

An astronomer at heart, the man pondered the tread-bare galaxy of the vulcanized surface, wondering how far it had drifted to enter this cosmological stew. As with the other worn-out objects in his carport, he could never bring himself to throw much of anything away. Family, neighbors, friends—virtually anyone who saw the tower of tires in their comedic baldness—ribbed him for it. He was able to laugh at his penchant for maximizing every millimeter of tread from a steel-belted radial, but in the end he never divulged his reasons for refusing to throw them away. He imagined the tires and sundry castoff objects as dwindling universes, each with histories of good use, now forgotten and unneeded. And who, in their right mind, could refuse them?

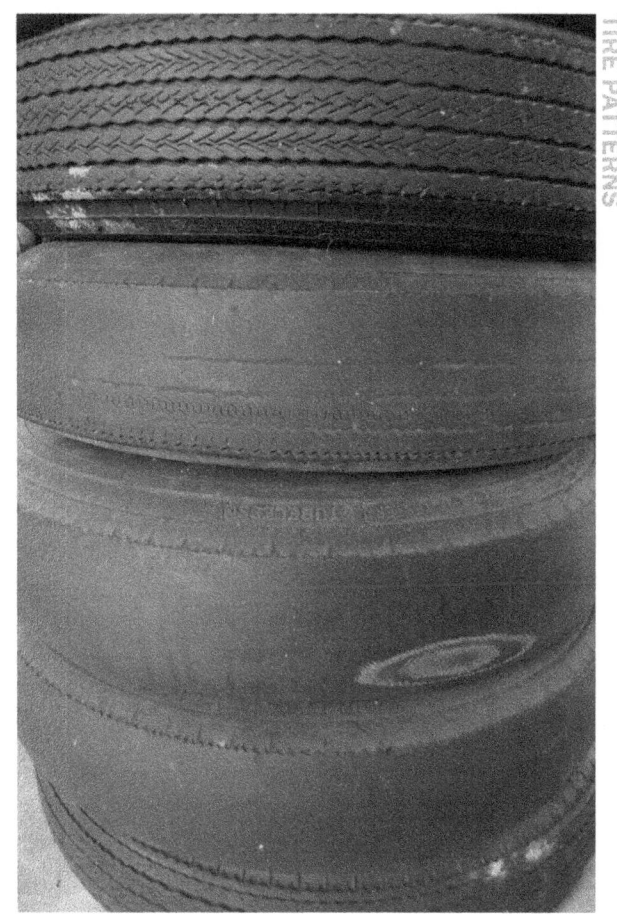

Baton Rouge, Louisiana   Nikon D40

On Mule Day 1911, while returning to the train depot in horse-drawn buggy, the President of the United States spontaneously requested repose here. An enormous man by choice, William Howard Taft walked unescorted to the water's edge where he stared out at the agitating surface, more likely staring inward at something stirring in his mind.

Placing his full weight on the bench, he leaned forward to scoop up handfuls of grit. Methodically separating rock from moist clay, he cast pebbles into the lake, each time wiping his hands on his tailored tweed slacks. His great size and station belied the truth—he was a child at play on the edge of the world.

Smack-dab in the middle of four uncomfortable political years, the president desperately needed a moment to be still, to be unbothered for once, to breathe air previously unbreathed by politicians. Wondering whether the outline of history would ever credit him for anything good, he recalled with joy his and Nellie's silver anniversary celebration earlier that summer. Rebuking the demands of time, reflecting on the beloved ones upholding his life, pushing back against pressing responsibilities, President Taft took solace in the miracle that there he stood, a man fully alive and breathing, casting ample reflection upon the earth.

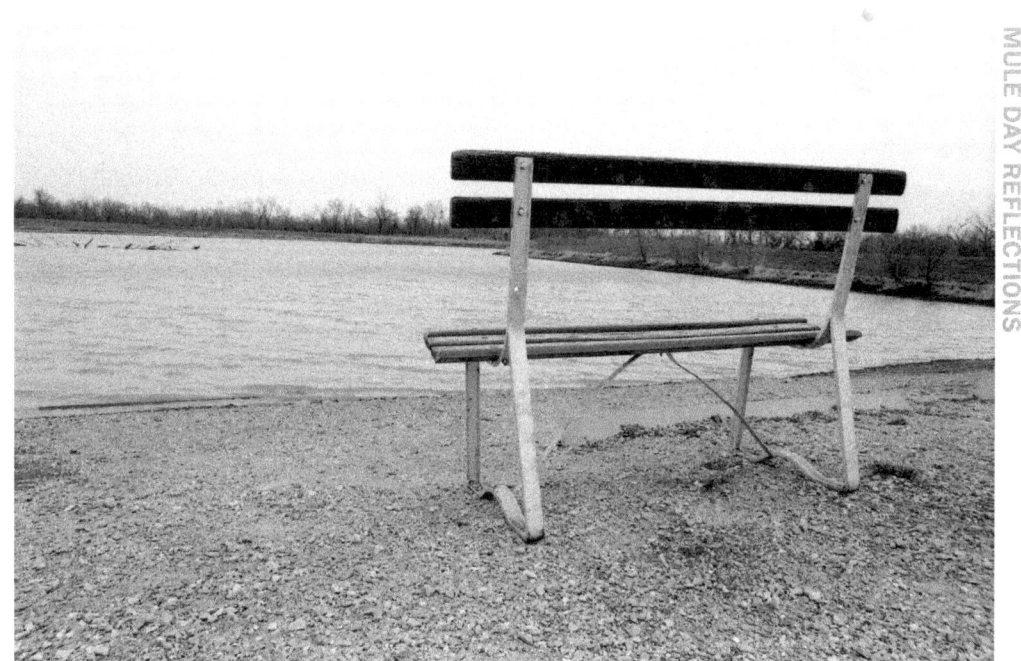

Sedalia, Missouri

Nikon D40

Your shoes are a half-size too small, and the fabric covering your preternaturally large right toe is worn thin, revealing the nail below. You are twenty-something, penniless, rarely content, hell-bent on conquering the world, and cocky enough to believe you'll do just that. You harbor a self-serving hope that this meek, odd-talking man with whom you've religiously crisscrossed the desert will, within your lifetime, literally rule the world. And you, his penny-pinching crony on a secret power trip, will receive a well-deserved appointment high up in the new administration. Attendant with such executive prestige will come a bloated salary to validate these three years of subsisting well below any Mediterranean poverty line of the day. However, it slowly becomes clear that the message he has been proclaiming, as opposed to the message you heard, are altogether different concepts.

A devout follower, ever pragmatic, you peer into the vapor trails littering the vast sky of your disappointment and mutter, "Who cares?" The endless journeying, the traipsing around for you no longer know what, the zealous devotion have all been for naught. Being a nobody was never part of your plan.

It's not that you are a devil of a person; having traveled far and wide, you've seen firsthand the unabashed darkness and treachery of man. Nor are you alone in your greed; you've seen far worse on public display. No, the issue is how you separate your ever-responsible, exhausted, striving self from that of Christ's beloved, and how you disconnect your disillusionment from the sin in your own veins. You are, after all, of practical mind. But practicality, when cast as a blanket, is a curse smothering an otherwise bright and significant heart.

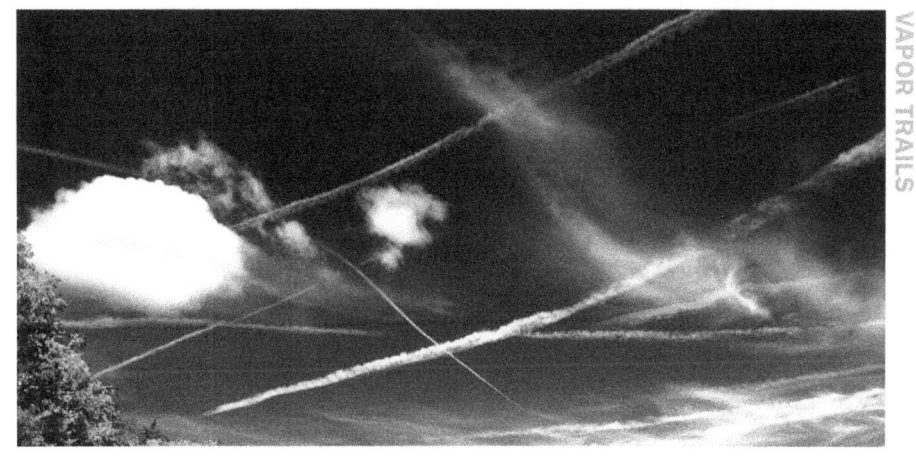

Nashville, Tennessee

Nikon D40

None of you suspected the evening would devolve into the final farewell it did—what with the tears of disbelief and suspicious glances. Judging by the table full of dinnerware, the twelve of you assumed you would be partaking in a celebration. The mood was light until Jesus, noticeably serene and distracted, cast a pall over the evening with all this morose talk of broken flesh and spilled blood.

For three years you heard him allude to a kingdom. You witnessed mirrors of moisture swelling in his eyes as he healed one sick person after another. But never before had there appeared such despair or anxiety. At the mention of betrayal amid the serving of bread and wine, something like guilt congealed and swept over you leaving you bereft of comfort. Casting his sad, gentle gaze about the room, you knew the jig was up, so you averted your eyes and feigned a cough.

From that moment on, death seemed your best and only option. So that is what you go and do: die everyday for the rest of your life. If only you had learned this lesson sooner.

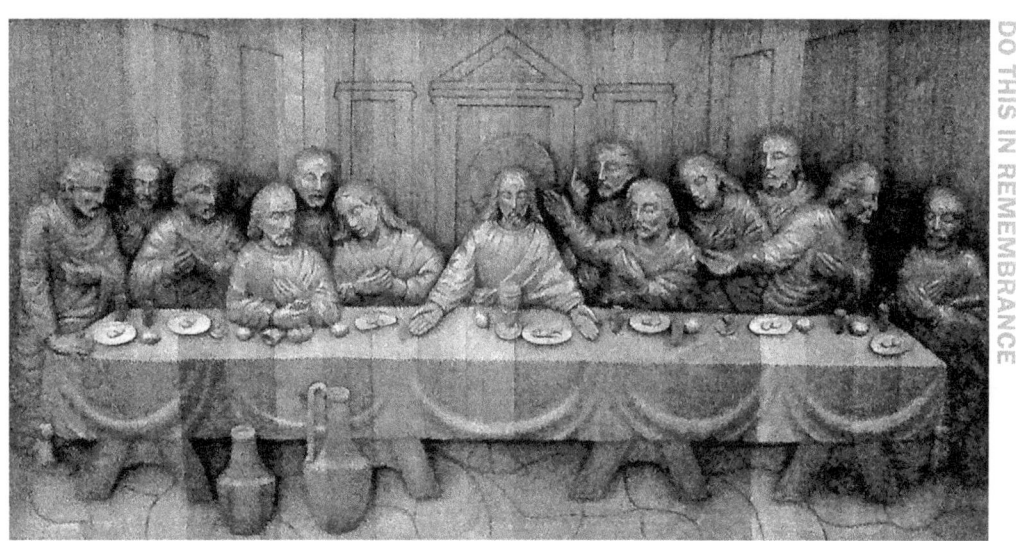

Nocona, Texas

Nikon D40

The habit of the soul is to believe itself a scourge, an unnecessary organism, a weed out of place in a victory garden. To release the work of our hands and minds into the world is ultimately the hardest act; that of relinquishing control. With no fanfare, and little aplomb except for the inherent joy of participating in rare moments of completion, we hold our breath and yield our art as it scatters beyond our protective reach, perhaps to resonate with earth, perhaps to shrivel in stony clefts, perhaps crushed under foot, or swallowed whole by wild things. Come what may—whether purchase or indifference—we continue to release ourselves because in the end, in the new earth, it is what we will do anyway.

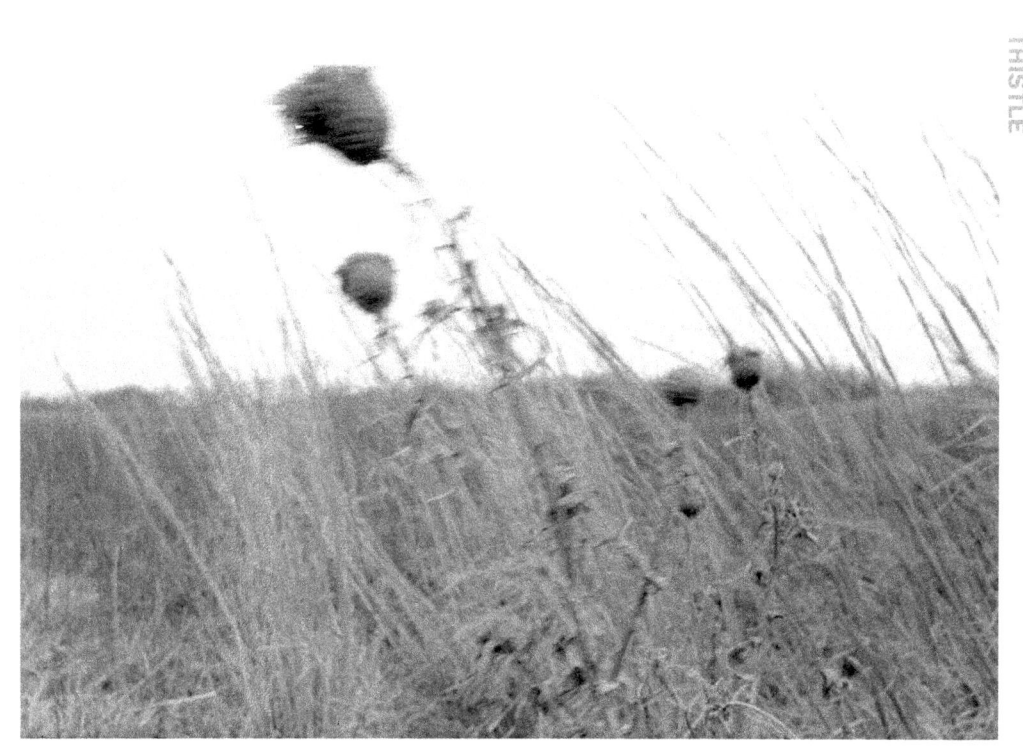

Vicinity Sedalia, Missouri

Nikon D40

Their paths happened to cross at the crest of the bridge where, in a deliberate attempt to gain her attention, the man timidly cracked a joke about a nearby brood of sunning red-eared turtles. She smiled, and conversation followed. She appeared from the trails through the boughs of Japanese maples. He appeared from Cullman County. Each, recently divorced, wading through the grief of lost time and failed relationship. For some reason, sharing such vulnerable information felt safe, necessary even.

Hobbyist photographers with K1000s in hand, they ventured to the garden that day in pursuit of vivid color. Perhaps what they needed more than anything else, more than the capture of still life on film, was to allow, like a released shutter, a pinpoint of another person's light and story into the paleness of their own grief, as if to remind them that not only were they not hobbyist humans, but they were not alone.

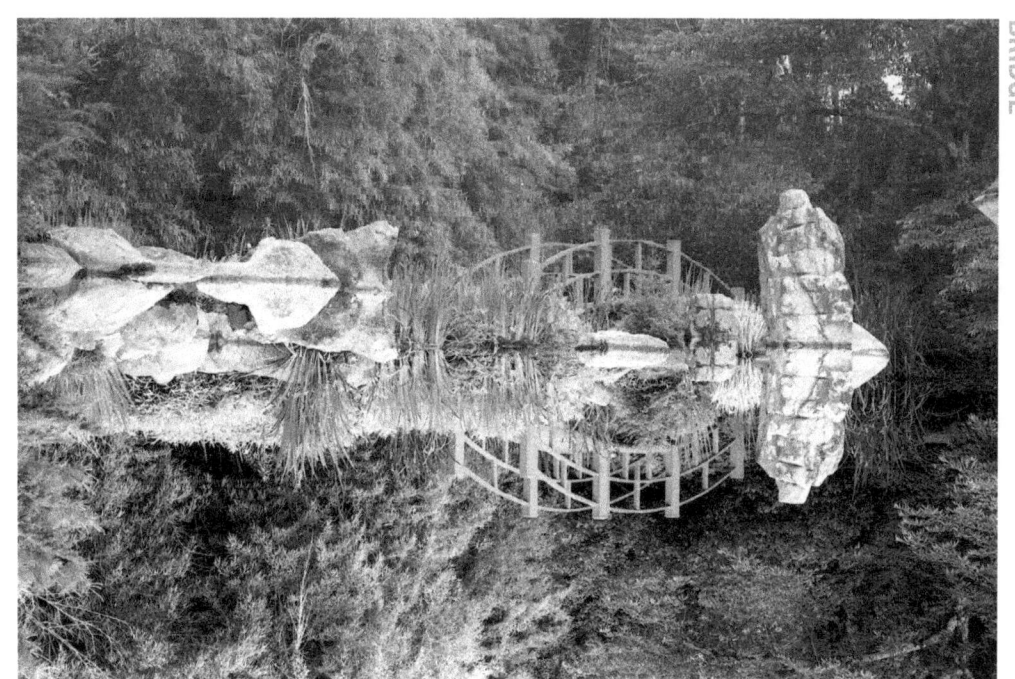

Birmingham, Alabama   Nikon D40

Knowing she had wanted, ever since childhood, a tree to call her own, the husband set about the task. The sculpture took him a year to complete, and in the end he painted it stark white for reasons even he couldn't articulate.

But she knew why: since Eve had plucked the forbidden fruit from the Tree of Knowledge, it meant the Tree of Life still stood somewhere in the world, overlooked perhaps, just as bright and permanent as ever. How badly she wanted to see it, to behold its eternal bloom, to swing from its branches. He could find no reason not to let her.

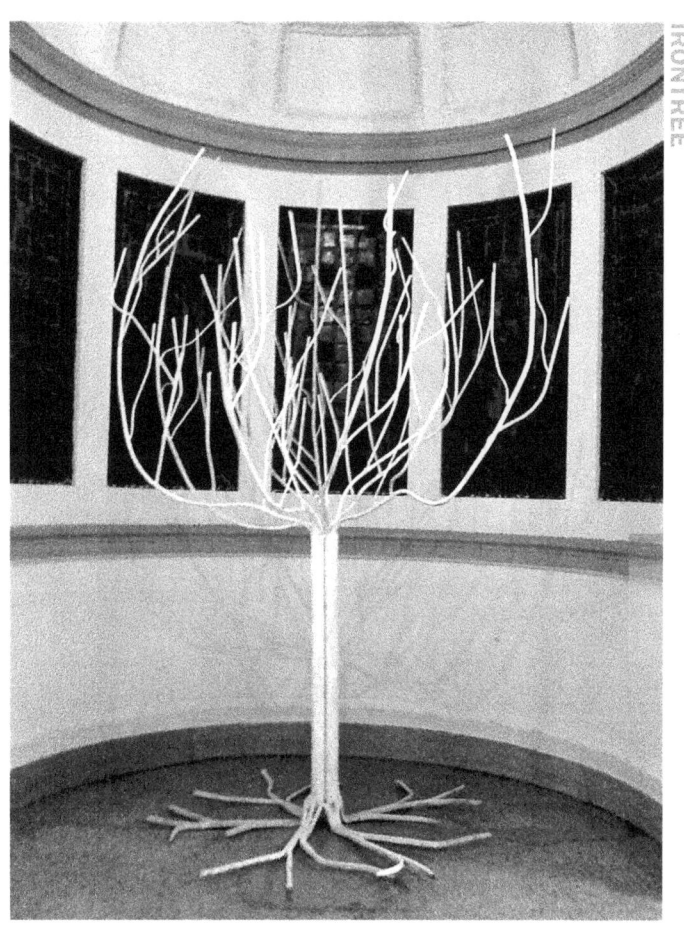

Charleston, West Virginia   iPhone

As did the fishing, the act of reading in his beat-to-hell, twelve-foot aluminum bateau brought him singular pleasure. Having witnessed the very same eccentricity in his father, it became the son's habit to stuff a novel inside the battery box where it could stay dry during the long float through duckweed and lilies. When the fish stopped biting, rather than retreat to the launch, he'd plunge a homemade, concrete anchor into the depths, or tie off to a tupelo. Opening a tepid cola and a can of Vienna sausages, he would, deep within the meandering, black veins of Bayou Sorrel, read aloud to the curious ears of the Atchafalaya watershed.

There was no haughtiness in the act, no elitist need to civilize the backwoods; he merely liked the sound of Dillard against the feathery backdrop of bald cypress, felt at ease in the reverberating echo of Stegner skimming like dragonflies across the water. As a child his father brought him along on fishing trips, and now, judging by the ensuing tranquility, he understood why.

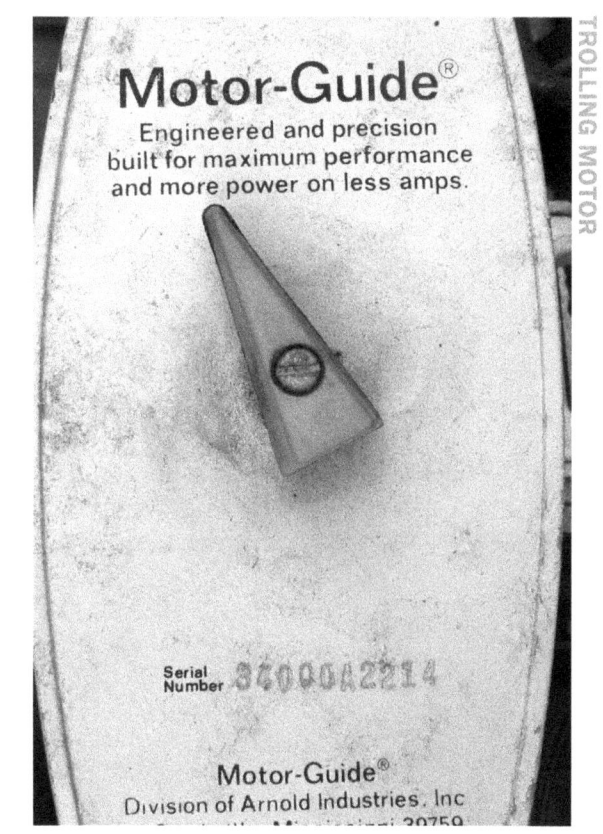

49

Expressing as much penitence as a deranged cat having taken a vehement swipe at its owner, the man and his machine leveled the former daycare. Construction takes time, time takes forever, but a man bearing a crowbar or a grudge can easily demolish it all.

Hauled away in numerous loads, the lot was at last emptied of debris and the one constant it had known: the sound of children. Once those old echoes faded, the land did the only thing it could: dream of new beginnings.

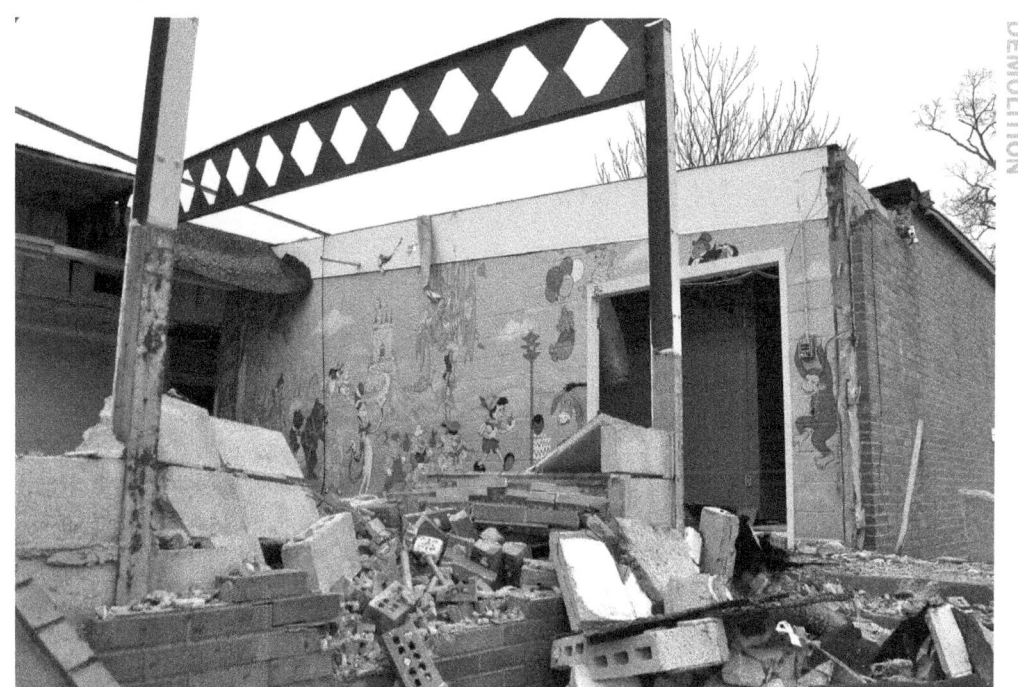

Nashville, Tennessee

Nikon D40

Slinking down against the wall at the painted boy's feet, the girl, her legs pretzel-crossed, pretended to read to him books she could not yet read. She appointed him her guardian angel, the only soul to whom she could divulge her unimaginable secrets. The angel and Eeyore, sad as always, listened.

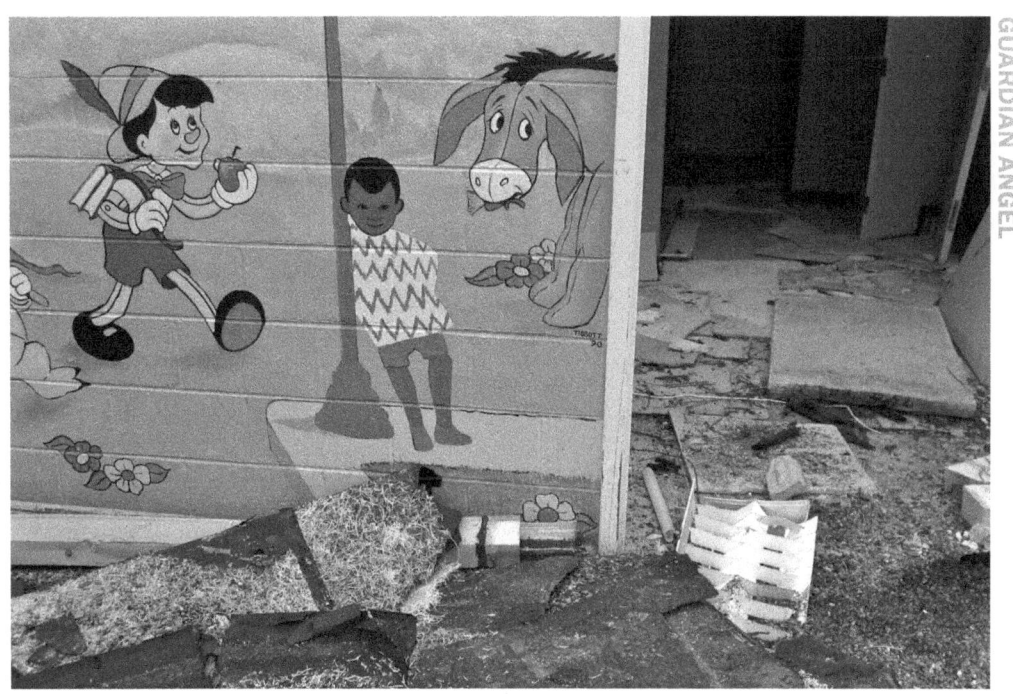

Nashville, Tennessee

Nikon D40

The price tag read fifty-five cents, but the shrewd owner had finagled the machine to require an additional dollar in order to dispense its more age-restrictive options. Only the owner and his regular, legal-age clientele were privy to Pandora's secret. A bored neighborhood teenager loitering outside the store one Saturday night lucked upon the riddle when, out of adolescent exasperation, he shoved a surplus of coins into the slot, and discovered that the vending machine worked just fine, thank you very much.

Shortly thereafter, the owner removed the mixed messages as well as the restricted contents, much to the chagrin of his regular, enlightened clientele.

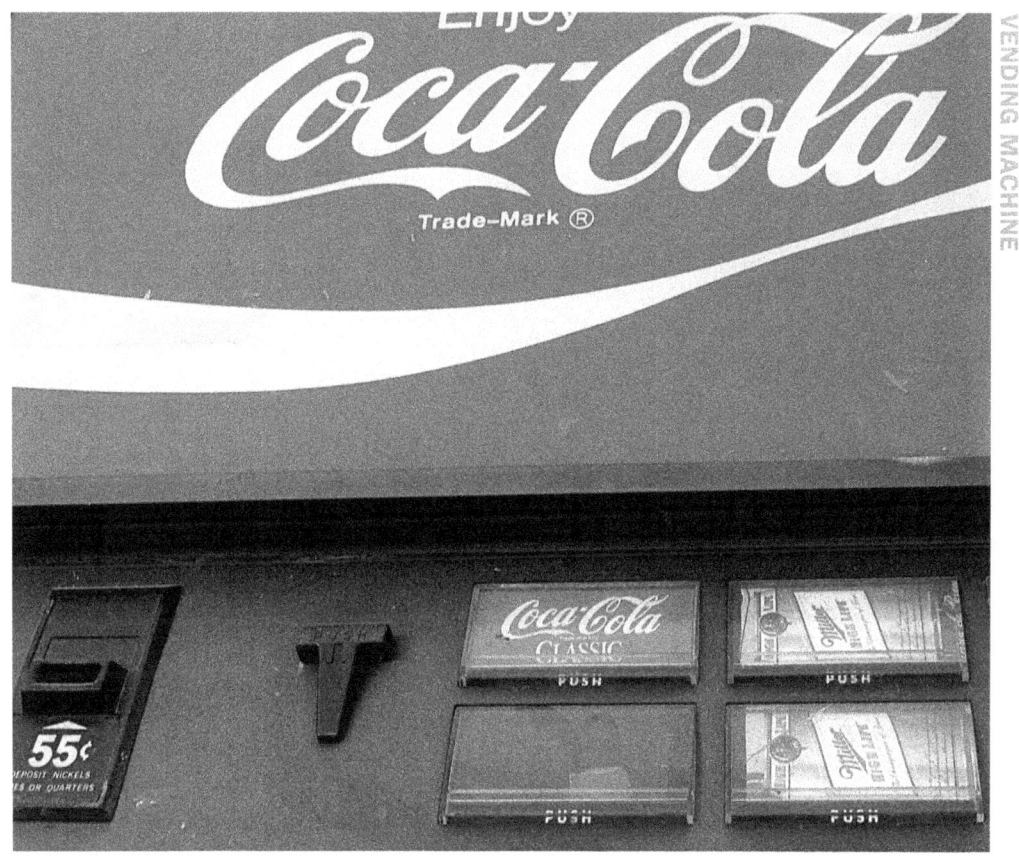

Baton Rouge, Louisiana

Nikon D40

He all of a sudden saw a blinding flash of stars. An astronomer all his life, this was neither a new nor an unwanted spectacle. After all, it was his life's ambition to witness celestials streaking across the sky. That they had fallen in complete disarray, leaving him disoriented on the ground was, however, worrisome. Being the first of an intensifying series of vacant spaces in his memory, he learned these absences had far less to do with near light than with an approaching darkness.

The blank spots grew, consuming more and more of his memory until he no longer recognized his own family or belly birthmark. Eventually he forgot everything, receding silently into the opaque sky of his terminal mind.

If only his loved ones were privy to his new cosmos, they might be comforted to know he was not lost forever inside a vacuous no-place. Though mourning on the losing side of loss, their memories of him are the only lights they have to fend off their collective sadness. Now, when they look up at the stars, seemingly overwhelmed by the black sky, they recognize traces of their beloved father. The darkness can never take that away from them.

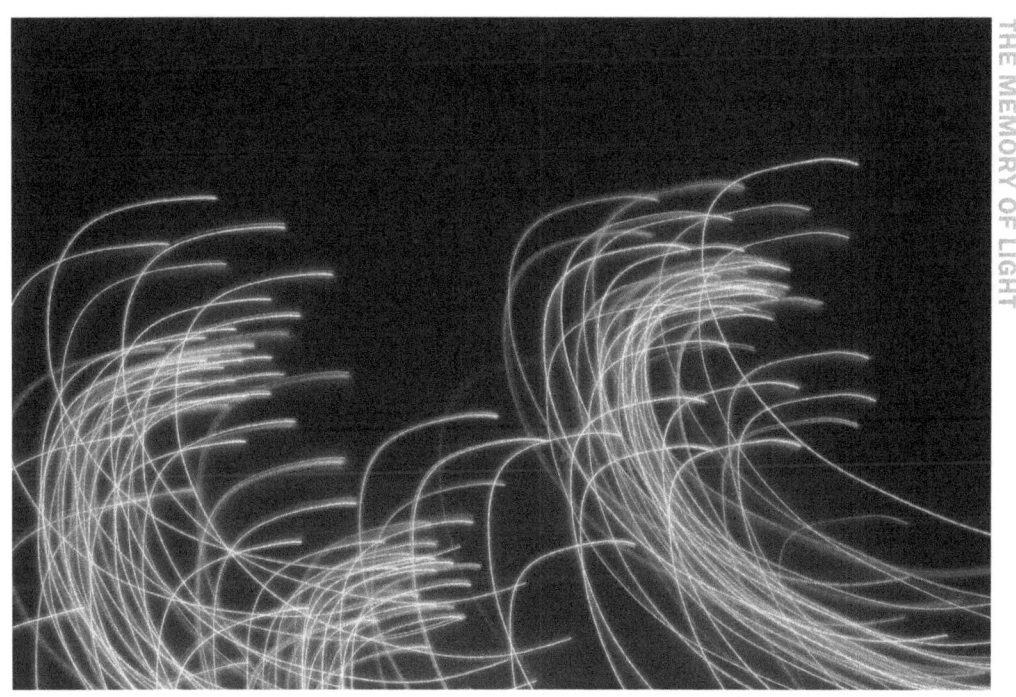

Nashville, Tennessee

Nikon D40

We venture apart, at times as far as one ocean shore is from another, yet at the end of the day we find ourselves together again, familiar strangers resting next to, leaning on, collapsing into one another. Through the years of innumerable and thankless labors, deflating moments, and mind-tapping exhaustion, we hold to the purpose of emptying our hollow selves, to serving one another. What God has joined together, let no man put asunder.

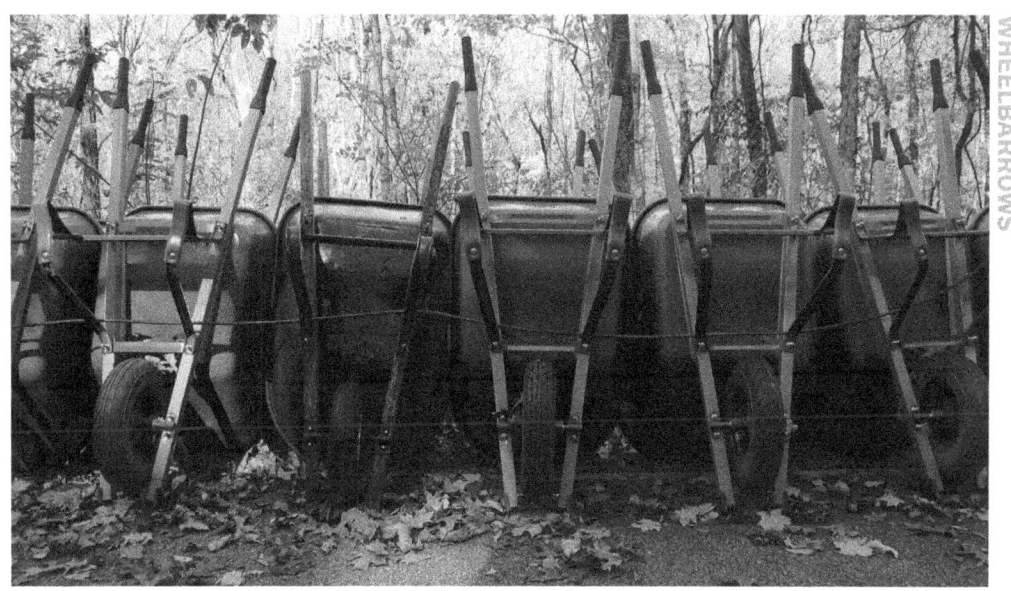

Nashville, Tennessee

Nikon D40

Pointing at the phantom ribs, he asked permission to touch and confirm that what he was seeing was real, to believe that he was real, not dreaming any of it. Possessing a hopeful though misunderstood faith, he had to not only see with his eyes, but feel with his hands in order to believe something with all his heart. With the curious and enviable faith children alone can express, he pressed his finger to the wounded void and, to his great embarrassment, he laughed. Surprised by joy and the unexpected mirth of being alive, he was affirmed that, however numerous and great, his doubts were merely fingers pointing to the bruised ribs.

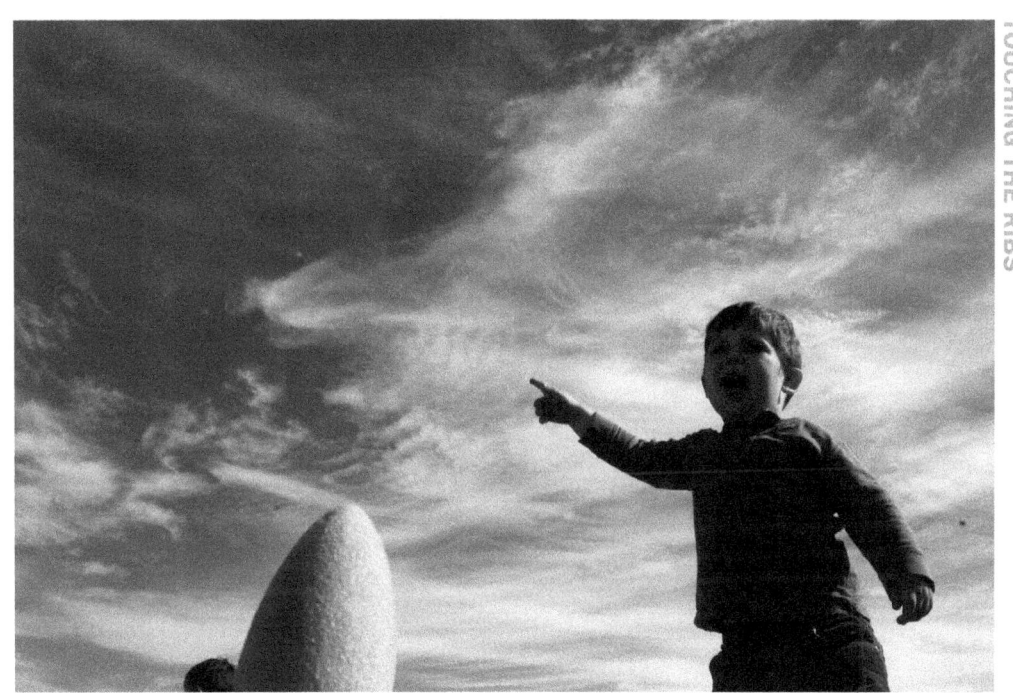

Baton Rouge, Louisiana

Nikon D40

From her kitchen window domain, perched next to a wall-mounted rotary phone, Lucille anticipated the mail delivery the way a child anticipates candy rewards. Most days it was the only noteworthy event to occur. In their golden years, she commandeered the routine from Wilton, insisting that he leave to her alone the task of journeying the fifty or so feet to their mailbox, itself impaled on a post poking out of the red dirt along Oral Church Road. His time and mind, in her opinion at least, were better off occupied by jigsaw puzzles, or by yanking swollen ticks off their sequentially-named pet mutts: Rusty I, II, III, IV. For her, the mail was an escape from an isolated, though not lonesome, existence.

The flag was raised as if to say, "Here I am. Take me." And that is just what happened to Lucille in the canned goods aisle of the local Sunflower grocery store. Without warning, she crumbled to the linoleum floor only to awaken in a new sanctuary—one free from vagaries and stifling kitchens. Fledging from her own nest, she was at last able to bask in the vibrant panoramas previously only seen in the strewn two-dimensional pieces of her husband's incomplete puzzles.

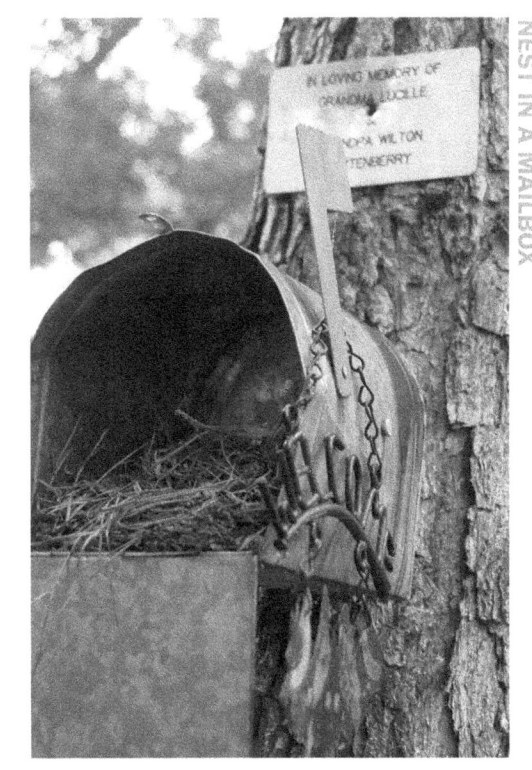

Tylertown, Mississippi   Nikon D40

On autumn evenings when the moon was full among the halo of stars, he relaxed by the fire, listening to the sounds of the surrounding forest. Eventually he drifted off to sleep in his chair, snoring beneath the nocturnal sky.

Now a grandfather, he recounts days past of great challenge and inner turmoil. He could never fully reconcile or quell the inexplicable anger inside him. There were times he adored parenthood and everything about it, while other moments he wanted nothing to do with the crushing burden of responsibility, or he wanted to retreat into solitude where no demands were thrust upon him, where no one would interrupt him, where silence was the norm, not the exception. He struggled mightily to control his temper and irritability, suspecting that his sons bore the price. He loathed himself for his weaknesses, for not being enough, for simply failing them. And yet, by apologizing, the man gave voice to something humble—a gentle, supernatural strength. Those words were a balm to the sons' singed hearts.

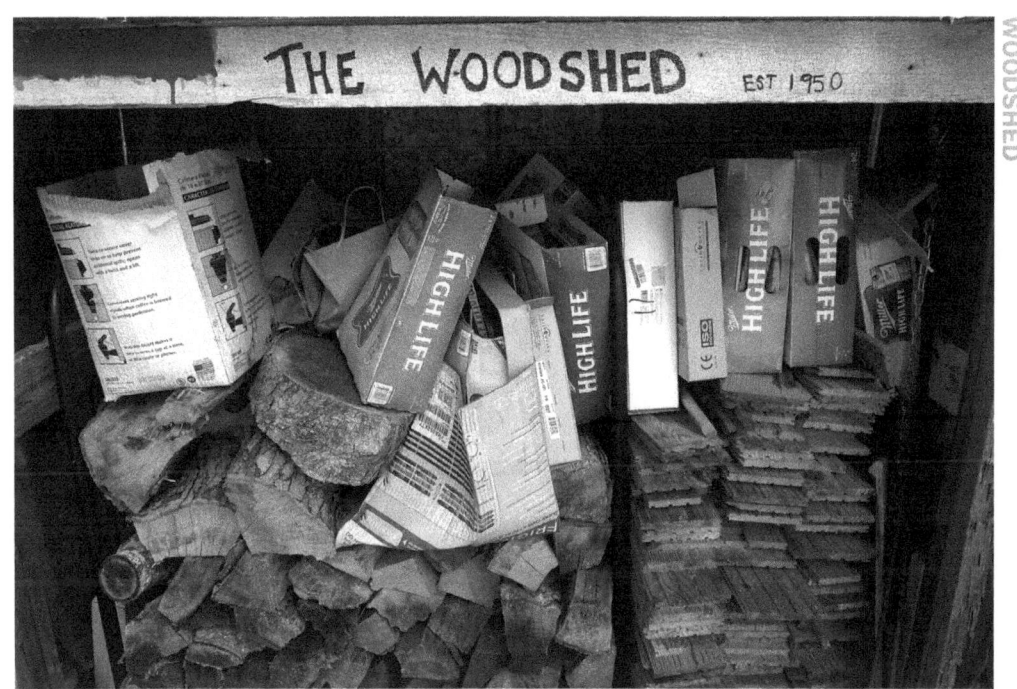

Tylertown, Mississippi

Nikon D40

The meter man was never without a pair of pruners or a pocketful of Milk Bone dog treats. The latter to win over menacing mutts standing guard in their yards, the former to clip Virginia creeper perpetually inching over the glass globe of the meter. At first, it annoyed him to have to trim the incessant new growth, but over time he settled into a rhythm, even liking the pause and creativity it required of him. Though not a self-described artist, he made an art of it, transforming the wall into a topiary, manicuring rogue shoots until he had trained it, as one would a pet, to grow around the meter, to take on new forms along the surface.

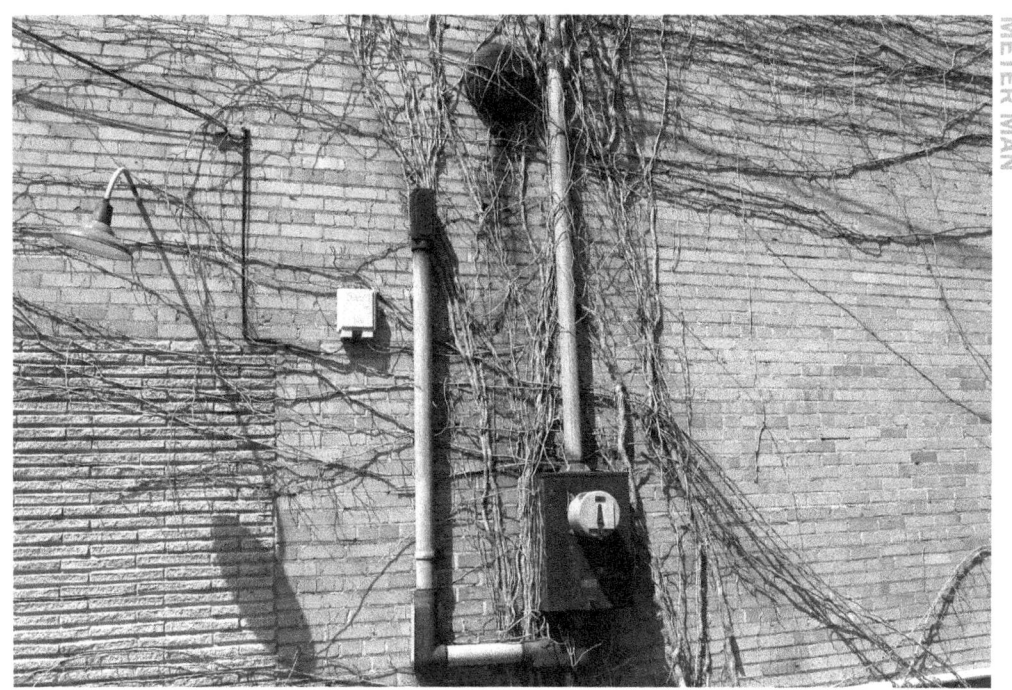

Tylertown, Mississippi   Nikon D40

The child's mother told her not to empty the container of chalk onto the pavement. The girl did it anyway. She did it not to be disobedient, but because that's what she and the smiling Trinity wanted, this act of emptying.

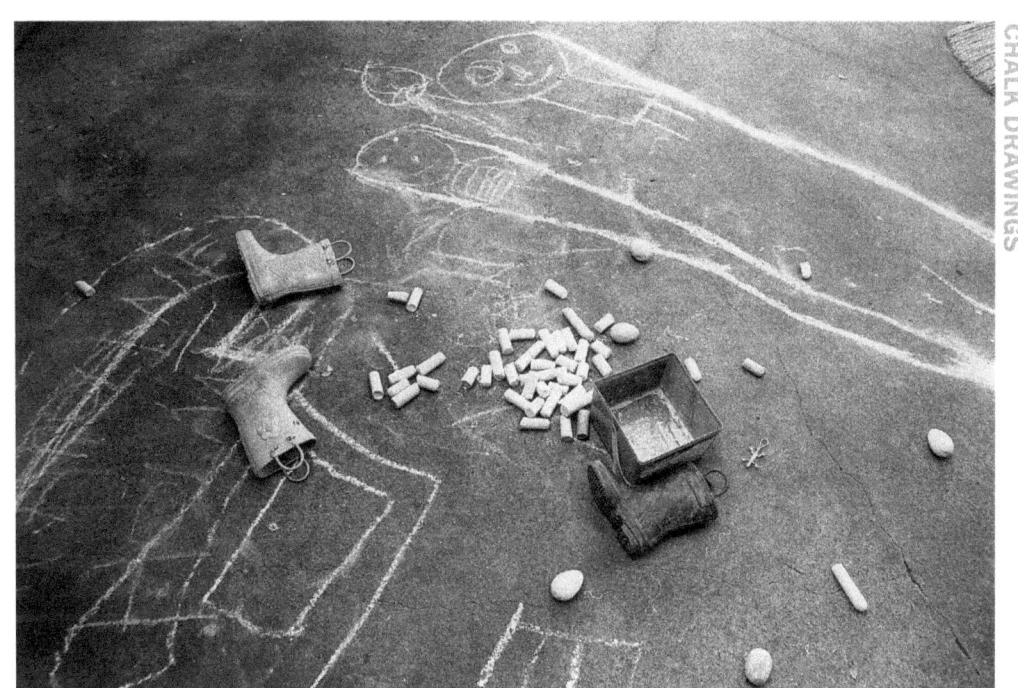

Dallas, Texas   Nikon D40

He imagined the sign's arrows pointing to the world's far off places. Like any teenager who ever lived the small town life, he too wanted to get out—but few ever did, or do, or bother to try.

Every so often the boy's parents receive a postcard in the mail. It bears no inscription, no news, just their scribbled names, rural route address, and a stamp placed upside-down in the lower left corner. The unorthodox placement of postage immediately identified the sender, and recalled to them their child's many eccentricities. Postcards were his way of letting them know his whereabouts, and assuring them that, though wandering, he was not entirely lost.

The boy figured the world needed to be known and explored from an upside-down, unconventional perspective.

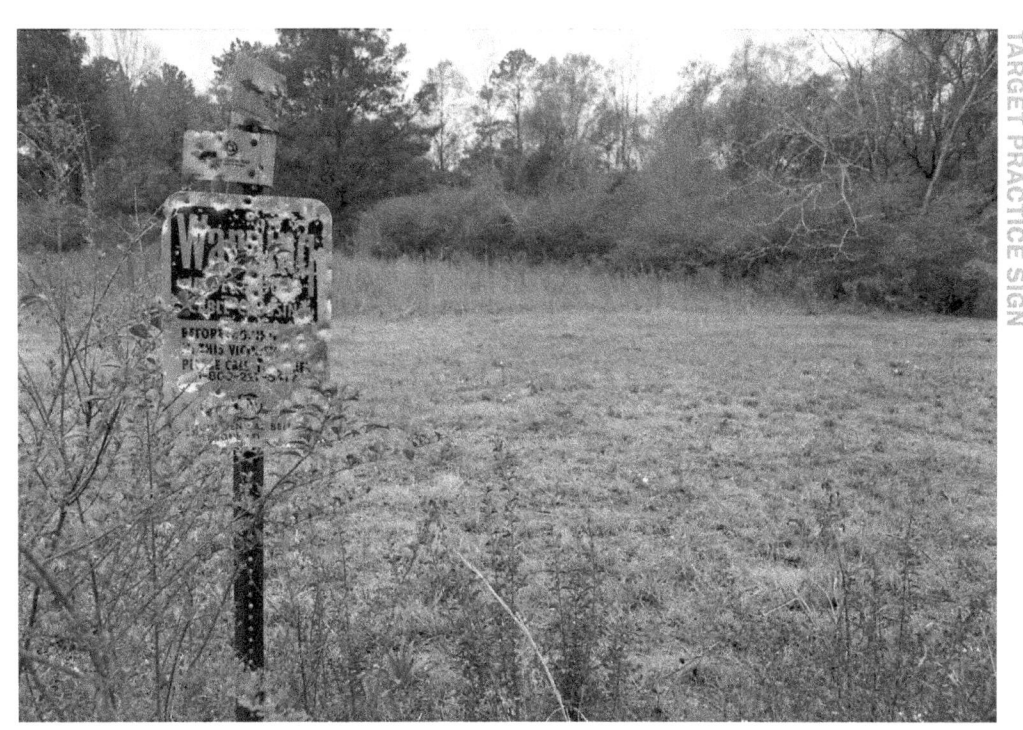

Vicinity Tylertown, Mississippi

Nikon D40

He entered the church only once after his family died in the accident. A farmer all his life, he was accustomed to being outdoors and working alone. Out in the open, feeling his chest release, he could breathe and let the work of his hands act as a metronome for the day. But now, inside his empty home, he was not prepared for the torturous aftermath of silence and loneliness.

The night of the death of his beautiful ones, he drove the seven dirt road miles to the plain church. Having practically grown up in this building, knowing the doors were never locked, his coming here was both an act of faith and one of refusal. His anger and confusion so intense, he was surprised to find he had to resist the urge to torch the place, to put a maul to its doors, to splinter its pews, to desecrate its baptismal water.

He never laid a vehement finger on the building that night, but he never forgot the desperation of wanting to tear the sacred things away from earth the way it had torn them from him.

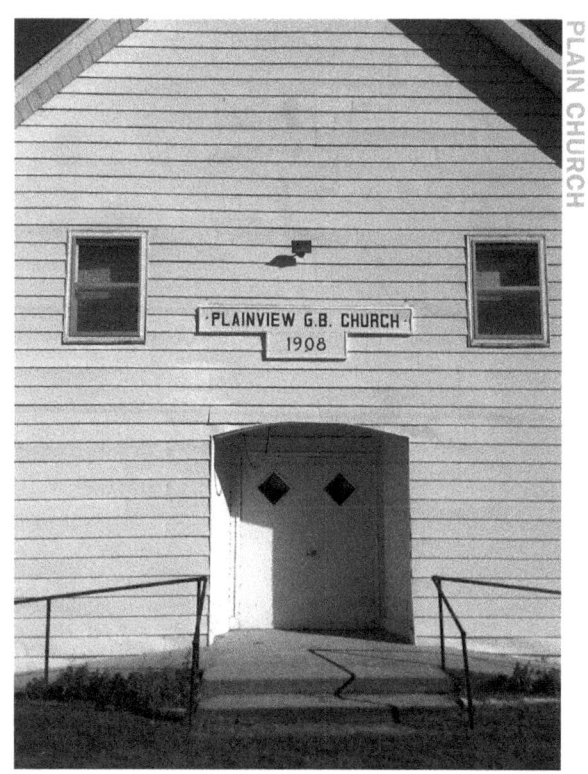

Vicinity Plainview, Illinois   Nikon D40

I worry over a world outside my realm of control: birds with no place to roost, venerable dogwoods showing signs of internal rot, weed trimmers flinging projectiles, children running recklessly by, leaf pools blurring the line between solid footing and slippery ground. I feel deeply. Heaven has yet to reject this.

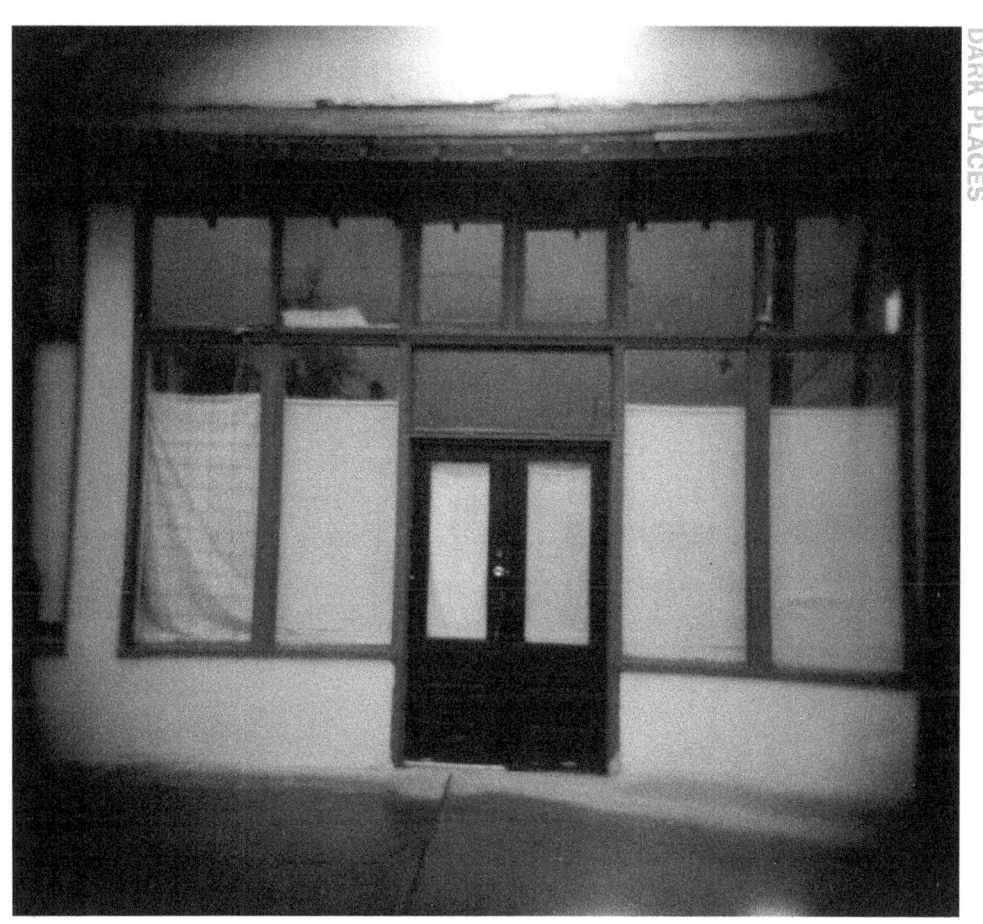

Nashville, Tennessee

Holga 120S

There was focus and purpose to everything the boy did. The bucket, intended to hold living water and the catch of the day, remained dry while the sweltering burdens of the world circled about his innocent, carefree shoulders. Eventually the droning earth will rage in his maturing ears, but he carries the trait of stubborn, dogged persistence. This quality will serve him well in life.

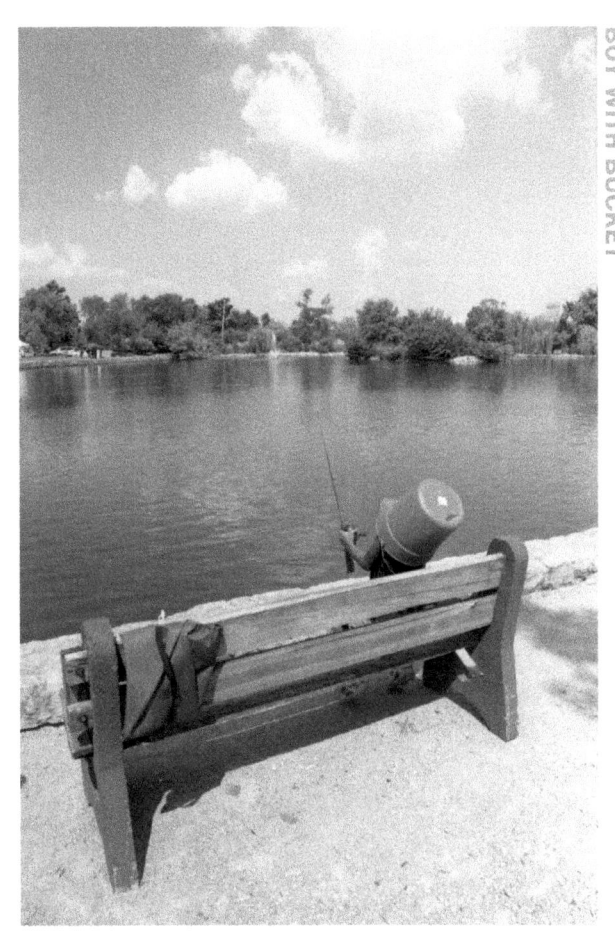

Nashville, Tennessee   Nikon D40

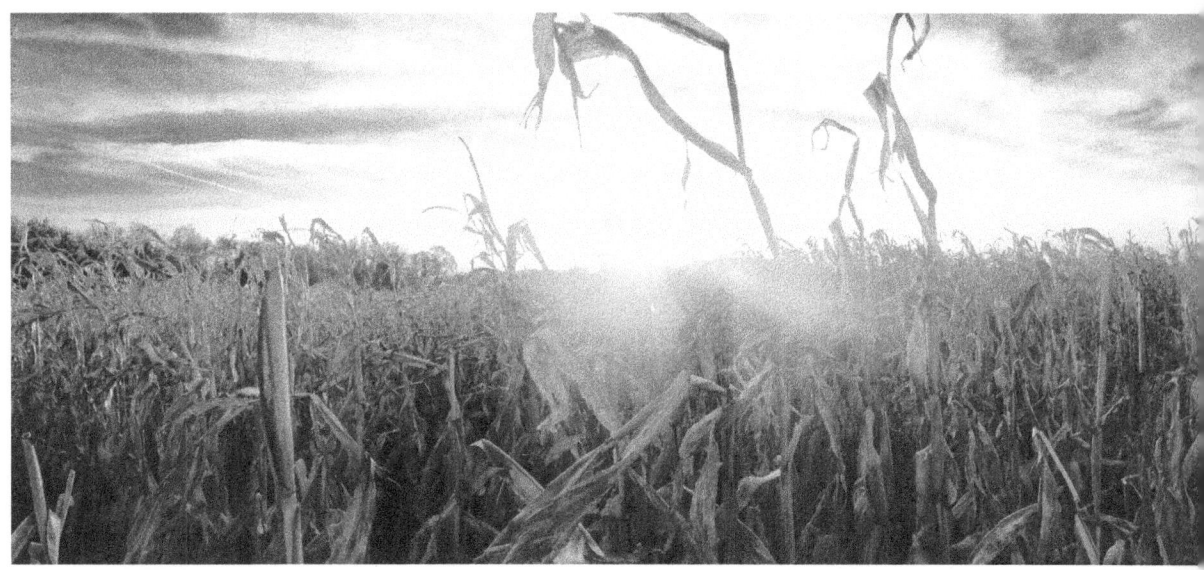

Bryant, Indiana

Crows scatter in flocks so big it makes me wonder whether they do it for scare tactic, from being startled, or from the sheer delight of being able to join the chorus of the sky, knowing full well the awe it evokes.

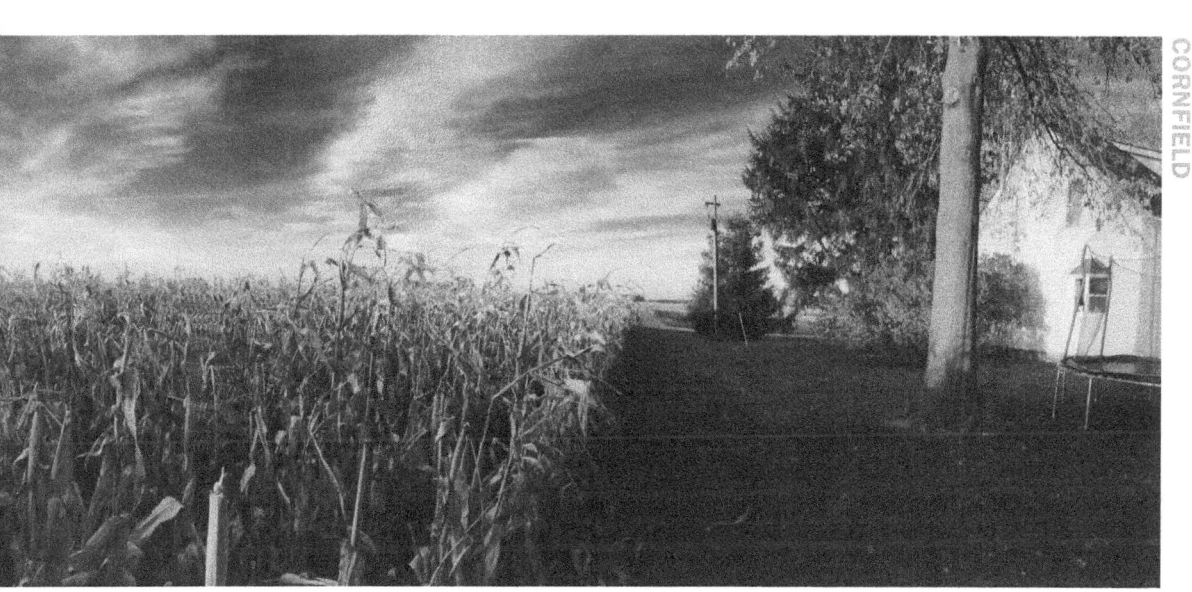

iPhone

In life, as in a double-exposed photograph, I am never certain whether I'm the image being haunted, or the one doing the haunting.

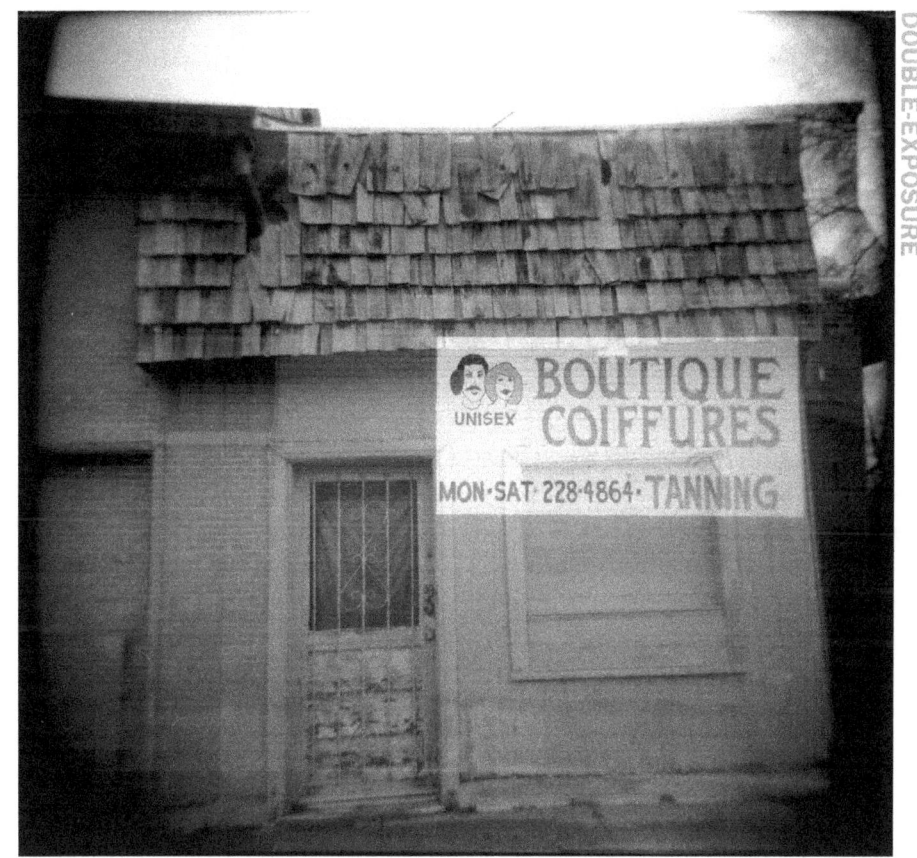

Nashville, Tennessee   Holga 120S

Spring arrived early the year I was chopped down. A pair of mockingbirds chose me to host their lively brood. I had done nothing to merit the grace, only offering myself.

We are Hallelujah Orphans, chosen in spite of status or strength, to herald, foster, and remember beauty by offering ourselves to an old Story. These small acts of remembering make visible again the invisible.

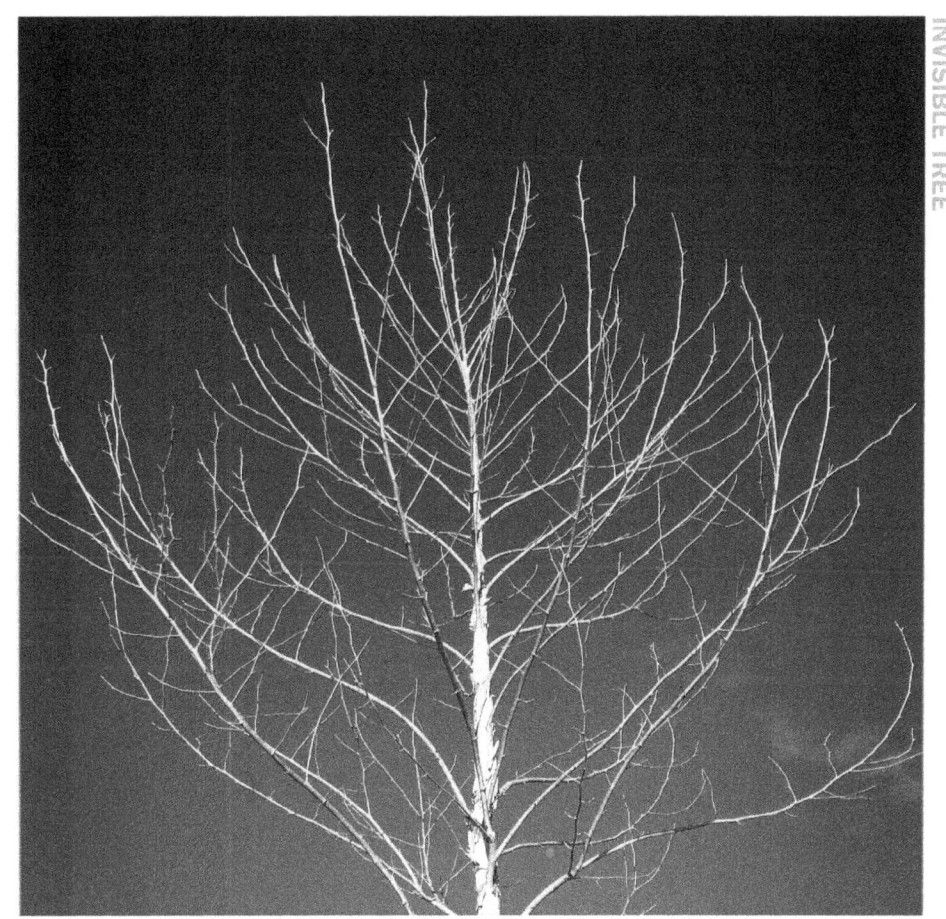

Nashville, Tennessee   iPhone

Two thousand pigs drowned in the sea that day. We saw them race down the bank in a frenzy as if chased by a legion of demons. We supposed the world was ending, what with the reprehensible sounds they made, the squealing chaos, and filth left in their wake.

Amid the sight and sound of all that bloated, reeking death, love chases away the loneliness until living is left in its wake.

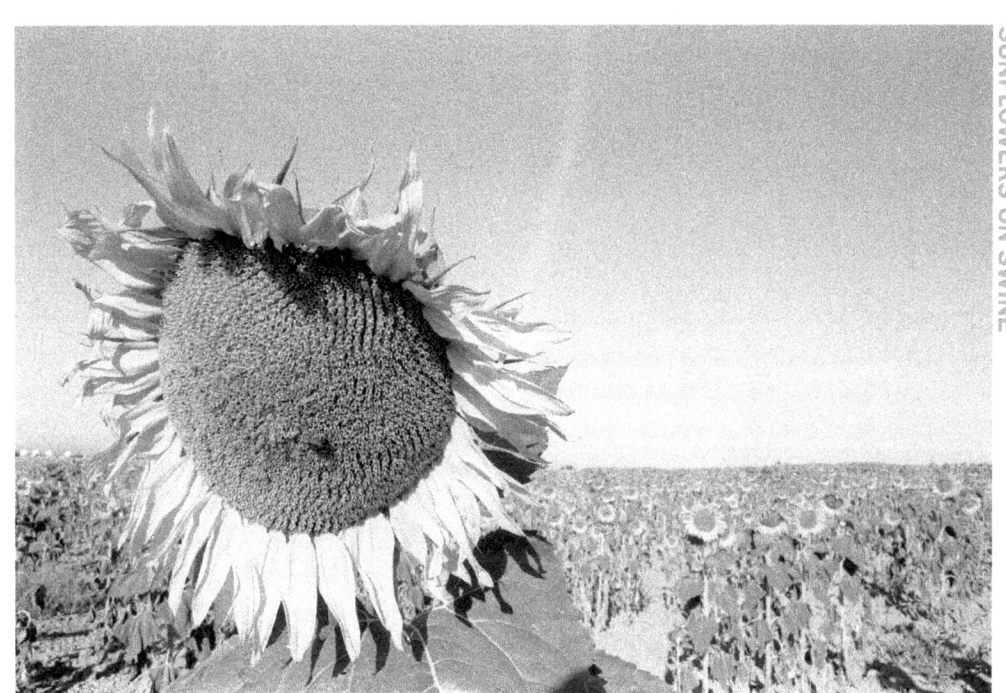

Eastern Colorado

Yashica 35mm

Storms balloon in the sky, lightning strikes, the world quakes, fears mount beneath hope's neglect and disappointment. Great waters bear the massive waves of the Redeemer's sufferings. Here, I can either live a death, or die one. His passion finds no fault, delivers calm from chaos, light from darkness, and life from dead, far off shores.

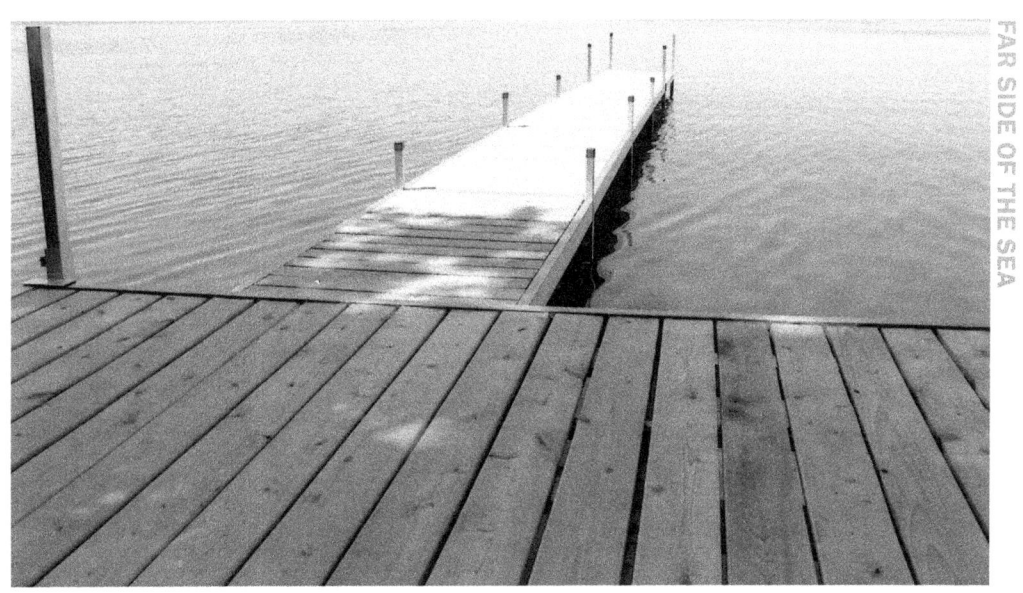

Detroit Lakes, Minnesota   Nikon D40

Photographs by Eric Peters using a variety of cameras:

35mm film, 120 film, digital, and smartphone

MUSIC BY ERIC PETERS

Earth Has No Sorrow: A Hymns Project (2020)

Far Side Of The Sea (2016)

Counting My Rings: B-sides (2014)

Birds Of Relocation (2012)

Chrome (2009)

Scarce (2006)

Bookmark (2004)

Miracle Of Forgetting (2003)

Land Of The Living (2001)

More Than Watchmen (1999)

The Only Thing (1997) (with Ridgely)

Ridgely (1995) (with Ridgely)

BOOKS BY ERIC PETERS

Far Side Of The Sea: A Photographic Memory (2016)

Revenge Of The Birds (2009)
(epic adventure space novella for children of all ages)

For more information visit www.EricPeters.net

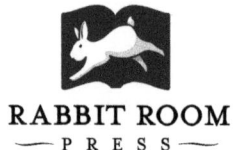

RABBIT ROOM
— P R E S S —